P9-DOH-551

Slowing Down to the Speed of Life

ALSO BY RICHARD CARLSON:
Don't Sweat the Small Stuff
Handbook for the Heart (co-editor)
Handbook for the Soul (co-editor)
Shortcut Through Therapy
You Can Feel Good Again
You Can Be Happy No Matter What

ALSO BY JOSEPH BAILEY:
The Serenity Principle

Slowing Down to the Speed of Life

---

*How to Create
a More Peaceful, Simpler Life
from the Inside Out*

**RICHARD CARLSON
AND JOSEPH BAILEY**

HarperSanFrancisco
A Division of HarperCollinsPublishers

SLOWING DOWN TO THE SPEED OF LIFE: *How to Create a More Peaceful, Simpler Life from the Inside Out.* Copyright © 1997 by Richard Carlson and Joseph Bailey. All rights reserved. Printed in the United States of America. No part of this book may be used or reproduced in any manner whatsoever without written permission except in the case of brief quotations embodied in critical articles and reviews. For information address HarperCollins Publishers, 10 East 53rd Street, New York, NY 10022.

HarperCollins books may be purchased for educational, business, or sales promotional use. For information please write: Special Markets Department, HarperCollins Publishers, Inc., 10 East 53rd Street, New York, NY 10022.

HarperCollins Web Site: http://www.harpercollins.com

HarperCollins®, ☰ ®, and HarperSanFrancisco™ are trademarks of HarperCollins Publishers Inc.

FIRST HARPERCOLLINS PAPERBACK EDITION PUBLISHED IN 1998

Designed by Laura Lindgren

Library of Congress Cataloging-in-Publication Data

Carlson, Richard.
      Slowing down to the speed of life : how to create a more peaceful, simpler life
   from the inside out / Richard Carlson and Joseph Bailey. — 1st ed.
      Includes bibliographical references and index.
      ISBN 0-06-251453-9 (cloth). — ISBN 0-06-251454-7 (pbk.)
      1. Time management.   I. Bailey, Joseph V.   II. Title.
   BF637.T5C37   1997
   158—dc21   97-5358

   99 00 01 02 RRD(H) 20 19 18 17 16 15 14

To Our Parents

CONTENTS

ACKNOWLEDGMENTS

—◆—

We would like to acknowledge the following people for their loving assistance in the creation of this book: Tom Grady of Harper San Francisco for his faith, enthusiasm, and creative editing; George Pransky for his helpful insights; Judy Sedgeman, Sandy Krot, and Rolf Schirg for their helpful and encouraging comments on the many drafts of the book; Michael Bailey and Kris Carlson for their loving encouragement and patience; the dozens of Psychology of Mind practitioners who have taught us so much about life; and the thousands of clients who have helped show us the importance of slowing down.

PREFACE

JOE'S STORY

In November of 1980 I attended a workshop entitled "Beyond Stress and Burnout for the Helping Professional" that would affect my life in ways I never dreamed possible. I was, in fact, feeling burned out by my life as a psychotherapist, seminar teacher, and nationally recognized leader in the addiction field. At the time, however, I thought I was just escaping the cold Minnesota winter to attend, in Miami, yet another workshop promising an answer to my stressed life.

Up until that point, I saw life as a series of tasks to get done, lists of items to accomplish, meetings to attend, activities to complete. I was almost always in a hurry, cramming as much as I could into a day. I thought this was the way to be happy. If I looked busy and important, I must be happy! Further, it seemed that all my friends, family, and colleagues did the same. It was hard to find a date on our busy calendars when we could get together, and when we did, we crammed as much activity into it as possible—jogging, eating, biking, and so forth. I looked like I had a full life, but I still felt empty, like I was somehow missing something. Maybe if I were more successful and efficient or took up yet another activity?

Until I learned about the approach to psychology that we will be describing in this book, I lived life like a hamster on the wheel, running furiously, in a hurry to get nowhere, but thinking all along that I was just about there. I had many stress-related symptoms—tension, headaches, stomach problems, chronic worry, insomnia. I thought this was normal.

When I arrived in Miami the weather was tropical, a sharp contrast to the Minnesota winter. I was greeted by friends whom I hadn't seen in a number of years. They seemed different—far more relaxed than I was and happy. I thought arrogantly, "They aren't as stressed as I am because of the intense demands of my schedule and my busy client load. Certainly, they must not be as important as I am." Everyone I was introduced to seemed so calm and happy and yet so ordinary. I was curious about why they acted this way. I soon felt comfortable with the new strangers in my life. This was in sharp contrast to the usual psychology conferences I attended, where everyone was serious, aloof, and busy trying to impress one another intellectually.

The first evening we had dinner at the home of one of the conference leaders. After dinner we were sitting around the room in casual conversation, when Syd Banks (the initial inspiration behind this form of psychology) began to speak. The audience listened with a deep respect, and the room became extremely quiet and calm. At first I was uncomfortable with the quiet feeling in the room and began to fidget. What he was saying sounded so simple, yet for some reason I couldn't understand it. My brain was swirling with confusion, doing inner battle both with his ideas and with the ideas I had been trained in professionally.

The next day I attended the seminar at the University of Miami Medical School, which was cosponsoring this conference for professionals who were shaping the new school of psychology that would later be named Psychology of Mind. There were psychologists, physicians, nurses, social workers, and representatives of many other professions—all as intrigued as I was with this new way of looking at mental illness, addictions, and other human problems. My confusion became even worse that day as my cherished professional beliefs were challenged one by one. I argued with the others about the simplicity of this approach, but at the same time I was absolutely fascinated with what I was hearing.

What I learned was that my enjoyment of life has everything to do with being "in the moment" and that the only thing that keeps me (or anyone) from being fully in the moment is our misunderstanding of the nature of our own thinking—how it pulls us away from the moment, confuses us, and stresses us. I realized that everything I ever needed is right here, right now—as long as my thinking doesn't carry me away from this moment. I learned that there is nothing in the future to rush off to that can offer me anything more than *this* precious moment that you and I are in every instant. I realized that, more often than not, my mind is somewhere else—a past regret or a future worry, anywhere other than right here.

My first reaction to this insight was to feel a deep sense of peace. I felt like I did in the happiest days of my childhood. I felt relaxed, at peace, fulfilled, satisfied. At the same time, however, this message made me uncomfortable for two reasons. First, it was too simple. The answer had been right under my nose all my life. Why had I been searching so hard and stressing myself out in the process? I felt stupid and foolish. Second, as a teacher in my field, I felt not only that I had misled myself by running on the treadmill but that I had done the same to hundreds of clients and professional colleagues as well. We had all been innocently searching outside ourselves for an answer to more time and more satisfaction, and we had it within us all along. The profound nature of this insight caught me by surprise.

I returned to Minnesota after the weekend and watched my life begin to change. At first I feared my reaction was just a "seminar high" and that it would pass after a few days. Quite to the contrary, however, the feelings of peace and relaxation strengthened as I began to see the response in my psychotherapy clients. My clients reported that I made more sense and that I was finally telling them something that could actually help them change their lives. Simultaneously, my personal life gradually began to change. I began to make the quality of each moment more important than getting things done, yet to my surprise I actually was able to get more done with less effort and more enjoyment.

Since attending that initial seminar in 1980, I have felt gratitude for the positive changes this insight has brought to my life and the lives of those I work with. Over the years since then, I have realized this simple insight again many times; each time it becomes more clear and affects my life in a multitude of ways. I had to hire more therapists and form a clinic to meet the growing demand of my practice. To my surprise, I was being asked to speak to national groups all over the country and to appear in the media. My first book, *The Serenity Principle,* has been read by thousands of addicts and alcoholics, and I receive letters each week from people whose lives have been touched. My work has become an absolute joy and privilege. I feel I can really help people and not hurt myself in the process. Fifteen years ago, I never would have imagined my life becoming so successful and satisfying.

MEANWHILE (RICHARD'S STORY)

I was extremely busy pursuing a life of what, in retrospect, can best be described as one continuous rush. I was driven, always in a hurry, and incredibly busy. I had a full-time client load and was also working hard on my Ph.D. in psychology. My life was consumed with collecting achievements and experiences, winning, and staying busy. I was running forty miles a week training for my first marathon and was engaged to be married to Kristine, now my wife of a dozen years.

In my spare time I organized food drives and did other charitable work. I enjoyed reading and had a few good friends. My intentions were positive, but my life was a mess. My schedule was so hurried, rushed, and filled up that I honestly don't know how I managed to get everything done.

Many years later as I look back in a calmer frame of mind, I can see that I wasn't as productive as I thought at the time. I appeared very busy because I was moving very fast, but in reality I wasted a great deal of energy. I had linked busyness to goodness and productivity. Like the proverbial hamster on a wheel, I was running fast but was only traveling in circles. Because my mind was spinning in so many directions and because I was in such a hurry to be anywhere other than where I was, I was a very poor listener. I would finish other people's sentences for them because I was not patient enough to let them do so themselves.

In the spring of 1985 my fiancée went to Portland, Oregon, to plan our wedding. I stayed in the San Francisco Bay Area to avoid a nervous breakdown. In those days, a single missed day of work was like a nightmare to me. Vacations, sick days, even family emergencies were seen as annoyances and tremendous sources of stress. Anything that interfered with my hectic schedule made me feel panicked and frustrated. Every minute of every day was filled up, and then some. It was at that time that I developed my habit of getting up at 3:00 or 4:00 in the morning to give myself extra time. "Most people get too much sleep," I insisted as I gulped down ten to fifteen cups of coffee per day!

I was often late to my appointments because I tried to stay to the last possible minute on whatever project I was working on. Every minute seemed to matter, but no matter how many minutes, hours, or days I had, it was never enough. Life was always going to calm down "later," when the important stuff was finished. The problem was, I looked at practically everything as important.

In August of that year my life suddenly changed. Our wedding was to take place on the last day of August, a beautiful time of year in the Pacific Northwest. Two nights before the wedding I received a phone call from my father letting me know of a great personal tragedy that affects me to this day. My best friend, Robert, and his terrific girlfriend had been killed by a drunk driver on a side road in southern Oregon. Robert, whom I had been friends with for most of my life, was driving north from San Francisco to be in our wedding party. I had spoken to him the night before the accident, and I remembered him saying, "Good-bye." I had no idea it would be for the last time.

We considered postponing the wedding but decided against it, as over three hundred people had traveled great distances to be with us. After a great deal of pain and sorrow, we managed to go through with the wedding, which included a beautiful, tear-filled moment of silence and a few words from a dear and trusted minister.

The tragedy became a major turning point in my life and changed my perspective in many ways. After the wedding, I began what has become a lifetime journey of deep reflection. Robert's death helped me to see the preciousness of life and the absurdity of the crazy pace at which most of us live. For the first time in my life I had been forced to slow down.

Ironically, Robert was one of the only people I had ever known who, even at a young age, had been able to live at what I now call a sane pace. He truly enjoyed his life. He had an easygoing way about him that allowed him to be relaxed and happy without sacrificing his ability to achieve. In fact, he was one of the most successful people I knew. Unfortunately, it took his death for me to fully appreciate the gifts he had been giving me all along.

As I began to slow down, my life began to change. My ability to focus on one thing at a time increased as I learned to dismiss the distractions from my mind. For the first time, I was able to stop working when it was time to do other things. At times, I was even able to do nothing at all, something that had previously been inconceivable to me. I appreciated life like never before, because my tunnel vision had been replaced by a broader perspective. Although at the time I didn't know what was happening to me, in retrospect I now realize that I was learning to live in the moment. Rather than constantly postponing my life, waiting until everything else was done in order to enjoy myself, I began to enjoy the very process of living. Instead of scattering my attention in ten directions at a time, I was able to focus intently, yet effortlessly, on whatever was before me—work, a friend, a project around the house, a book, preparing a meal, a conversation. As a result, my world began to come alive. Both my wisdom and my gratitude began to flourish. Because I was more present, I became more compassionate to the needs and struggles of others. I'm embarrassed to admit it, but prior to my change of heart I would organize a food drive, in part, to see whether I could create the most successful food drive around. After my change of heart I would organize a food drive because people were hungry and needed food.

Aspects of life that I had taken entirely for granted became sources of interest and joy. My ability to feel satisfied with my life increased. In short, my ordinary life was becoming extraordinary. Ironically, although I no longer felt as rushed and panicked, I became more productive than I had been. I was able to do more things in less time. I was less distracted by my own crazy thinking and worries, which freed up sources of creative energy that I had never before tapped. I began my writing career, which was ironic because writing takes an enormous amount of patience, something I lacked before Robert's death. Whereas before I had been like a race car speeding down the fast lane, never looking at or even noticing the view, I now felt like a car gliding down a country lane, taking in the scenery while still moving toward my destination.

Because my eyes had been opened to a better life, I became increasingly interested in helping others do the same. I wanted to teach people to experience my new outlook without having to go through a personal tragedy or crisis.

Shortly after this major turning point in my life, I was exposed to the material you will be introduced to in this book. An even brighter lightbulb went off in my mind.

Almost immediately, my understanding was enhanced, and for the first time I was able to put into words what I had been introduced to through tragedy. The understanding called Psychology of Mind gave me a context for grasping the profound insights of my experience. As you read this book and live your life, you will learn that these insights naturally occur to many human beings every day but often go unnoticed and unappreciated for their value in living a mentally healthy life. After my experience, everything was becoming clearer and life was becoming easier. It was at that time that I met Joe Bailey, co-author of this book, and together we explored and opened ourselves to aspects of life that were previously hidden from our awareness.

As the years have gone by, I have discovered that it's not only possible but actually quite simple to live at a slower, more manageable pace, a pace that allows you not only to excel in your achievements and goals but also to enjoy and appreciate every step of the way.

When Joe and I met we experienced an instant connection that has turned into a lifelong friendship. As you can probably sense from reading these first few pages, we had a great deal in common regarding our speeded-up tendencies and our awkward attempts to overcome them. Fortunately for the two of us, as our understanding of life has evolved, so too has our friendship. As we reflect on our own journeys, we sometimes chuckle at the way we used to live. Today, our commitment to a quality life and to helping others is as genuine as was our craziness of years past. We suppose it was only a matter of time before we put our heads together to share our vision and method of slowing down to the speed of life.

Last summer, the two of us were in Cambridge to attend the fifteenth annual meeting of Psychology of Mind. As we reflected on our own lives and on the insane pace of the world we now live in, it was apparent to us that a book on how to slow down to the moment and enjoy life was a project worth doing. As we ate dinner, a memory came to Joe from a client some years earlier. Joe had asked him, "How has your therapy helped you?" The client paused and then spontaneously answered, "I guess I learned how to slow down to the speed of life." We both knew this summed up the message we wanted to convey in this book.

As you begin to read this book, at first it may seem simplistic, unrealistic, or even Pollyannaish. If so, don't worry! This was true for us as well. To us, life seemed complex and overwhelming; a stressed life seemed normal and even healthy, given the state of our world. Be patient, however, and read on. Discover for yourself that life can be enjoyable, that it can be easier than you imagined, and that it can actually slow down to a very sane pace. It is our most sincere wish that you too will be able to slow down to the speed of life. If you can, the quality of your life will be greatly enhanced.

INTRODUCTION

Despite our best efforts to manage our time efficiently, and despite the many time-saving devices designed to make life easier, our lives often seemed filled to the brim. We cram our days with activities, thinking that each one of them is important and absolutely necessary. We schedule virtually every minute of every day. We say we want free time, but few of us can sit still, even for a moment.

Like our computers, we become adept at multitasking, juggling three or four tasks at once, with no room for error in any of them. God forbid the car phone should break down on the way to the office. If it breaks, you can't notify your East Coast office that the document you sent via your car fax is on the way.

For most people, such time savers as computers, fax machines, overnight delivery, voice mail, on-line services, or high-speed modems actually create more time stress than they eliminate. We may save time by making a ten-minute call on the car phone instead of talking on the home phone after dinner. But then, after dinner, we go ahead and make another call, losing the time we worked so hard to save. Instead of accomplishing the same goals more quickly, we set higher goals, constantly pushing ourselves to do more and do it faster, thus getting further and further behind. Where is all the time that we saved? When do we get it back? When do we get to enjoy life? Isn't that allegedly why we are doing all these things?

Unfortunately, the problem reaches far deeper than the misuse of time-saving gadgets. The feeling of being rushed saturates our entire way of life. We measure our success in life by our level of efficiency and our ability to stay on top of it all. We measure the health of our economy in terms of increasing productivity. Many of us unconsciously are indoctrinating our children into our "squeeze it all in" mentality. Besides learning how to read and write, very young children are involved in tennis, swimming, music, gymnastics, ballet, and soccer—often all at the same time, back to back, hour to hour.

When you slow down to the speed of life your perception of the world will change. It will become healthier and easier. You will work more intelligently and wisely than before. You will realize that much of what you previously thought was essential is actually unnecessary and can be postponed, delegated, or even disregarded. Living at the speed of life helps us set priorities in our lives in a more effective and joyful way. Instead of waiting to enjoy our lives when everything is finally done (which it never is), we can learn to enjoy the journey rather than merely looking forward to the final destination.

This is a book about slowing down and learning to live in the moment. We are not, however, going to ask you to change your lifestyle. You don't have to move to the country or to a small town in another state. You don't have to resign from your job or change your career. You don't have to stop watching television, avoid traffic jams, cancel all social engagements, or travel to India. We're not even going to ask you to take a pill or quit drinking coffee!

Most people who try to slow down put the proverbial cart before the horse. They make dramatic, often costly changes in their lifestyle, only to encounter two disappointing results. First, they don't enjoy the changes they make. People who are temperamentally used to a fast-paced life quickly discover that a slower-paced life in the country all but drives them crazy. Their habitual, frenzied thinking won't allow them to adjust the superficial changes they make. Second, lifestyle changes alone rarely make a real difference. You can rearrange the externals of your life in a radically different way, but you always take your thinking with you. If you are a hurried, rushed person in the city, you'll also be a hurried, rushed person in the country.

In this book, you will learn to slow down your life from the inside out. This change will result from a wiser way of being in the world, not from superficially reorganizing the externals of your life. You will discover how your quality of life is created within rather than imposed upon you by outside forces.

Of course, it's possible that after you learn to live in a calmer state of mind you may very well decide to make some lifestyle changes. If you do, you can be assured that you will enjoy the changes. They will serve you well because they will spring from a more intelligent understanding of life rather than just being another gimmick to help you cope.

The approach to slowing down that you will encounter in this book is based on a set of principles known as Psychology of Mind, which was initially inspired by a man named Syd Banks and was formulated into a psychology by Dr. Roger Mills and Dr. George Pransky.[1] The Psychology of Mind, or POM, is being used by a growing number of therapists, consultants, and educators throughout the country and around the world—with spectacular results. These ideas are simple, yet profound, even revolutionary. Inner-city public housing projects are being transformed, stay-at-home moms are learning to relax around their kids, and CEOs of giant corporations are running their companies at the speed of life with far greater ease and productivity.

What you will learn here has been extrapolated from the principles of POM in a way that is geared toward freeing you from the pace of our harried world.[2] Before we embraced these principles, we were no different from anyone else. Our inner worlds (our thoughts and feelings) were full of anxiety, worry, pressures, and a feeling of being overwhelmed by life's day-to-day problems. We had stomachaches, headaches, backaches, and other symptoms typical of our stress-filled world. We were convinced that if we just worked a little harder, faster, or more efficiently, we would somehow get ahead of the game and have time to relax. Like many, we lived in constant anticipation of the end of the day, the upcoming weekend, the next vacation; we even dreamed about quitting

---

[1] Interested readers can learn more about Psychology of Mind by writing to either of the addresses listed in the Resources section of this book.

[2] In addition to our own two books based on Psychology of Mind, *The Serenity Principle* (Joseph Bailey) and *You Can Feel Good Again* (Richard Carlson), there are several other excellent books available, including the primary resource book on POM, *The Renaissance of Psychology*, by Dr. George Pransky.

it all and traveling around the world. We fantasized about an illusory time of peace in the future that somehow never arrived.

At some point we began to realize that the world was not going to accommodate us by making fewer demands. We each learned that our inner experience of stress resulted not from the circumstances of our harried lives, but from our habitual way of perceiving life. We learned that we could change our inner worlds—our feelings, our stress levels, even the speed of our lives—by tapping into a way of thinking that makes life easier, simpler, and much more enjoyable. Many years later we continue to rediscover the practical and far-reaching implications of this initial understanding for our lives and the thousands of clients whose lives we have touched.

As practitioners of this psychology, we have spent many years teaching the principles we will describe in this book. As a result, many people around the world have learned to take control of their lives instead of feeling victimized by them. If you approach reading this book with an open mind, you too will learn:

- To slow down and enjoy each moment.
- That slowing down doesn't involve major changes in your lifestyle.
- That contrary to conventional wisdom, your productivity will actually increase when you slow down to the speed of life.
- That other people's habits, attitudes, behaviors, and moods don't have to affect the quality of your day or the speed of your life.

- That even though people around you or your work setting may be rushed and stressed, you can maintain a calm in the midst of their storm.
- That by slowing down to the moment, you will be far more prepared for the unexpected.
- That ordinary moments can become extraordinary.
- That even life's most serious circumstances and events don't have to be taken so seriously.
- That the best preparation for the future is to live your life fully in the present.
- That you can finally get the satisfaction you've been striving for.
- That, finally, you can be happy!

By picking up this book, you've taken the first step toward realizing these promises in your own life. The best way to read this book is to approach it with an open mind. See whether the ideas resonate with your own common sense on an intuitive, nonanalytical level, but try to avoid fitting the information into something you already intellectually believe. If you can digest and take to heart the information in this book, you will feel yourself slowing down right away. Very little effort will be involved.

This is not a book on "one hundred ways to slow down your life." In fact, you will notice early on in the book that we don't provide you with lists of things to do, exercises to practice, or suggestions on how to cut back your schedule or manage your time more efficiently. The reason is because, optimally, the feeling of slowing down is a qualitative experience that comes from the inside out, a way of relating to life that stems from a new understanding. After reading this book you may discover, as many others have, that most attempts to slow down your life from the outside in are superficial, at best. They provide temporary relief, a vacation from reality, but not a permanent change in the way you see life.

As you read through the book, you will begin to see the compelling logic of its message and the obvious truth of its principles for your life. Take your time to digest each moment as you read, and you will discover that never again does life have to become one big emergency. Slow down and enjoy.

CHAPTER 1

Slowing Down to the Moment

As young children we were full of life, always playing or running around with our friends. We would turn from one activity to another with endless enthusiasm. Games of hide-and-seek were an opportunity for unlimited imagination, exploration, and curiosity. It seemed we never got bored or tired of whatever we were doing in the moment. For the most part, our childhoods were an endless series of positive feelings—joy, laughter, curiosity, surprise, confidence, and adventure. We had not learned yet to worry, to hold grudges, or to have regrets about the past.

Most young children, in fact, are generally unstressed, full of awe and curiosity, and rarely bored. Most have enormous amounts of energy, are unconditionally loving, and seem to have boundless energy that make adults envy their innocent approach to life. These uncontaminated children live from a state of mind that we practitioners of Psychology of Mind like to call mental health. They live naturally in the moment.

As adults we still have the capacity for mental health, but we have been socialized into the busy ways of Western culture, and many of us have grown serious, analytical, stressed, depressed, and unimaginative. Beginning when we reach age five or six, and steadily progressing into adulthood, our experience of mental health declines. This decline seems to correspond with our propensity to use memory and analytical thinking more often as we get older and our creative, in-the-moment thinking less often.

As you will see, it is not only unnecessary but actually unnatural for human beings to lose this experience of mental health. It is only through a lack of understanding about the nature of our psychological functioning that this deterioration occurs. Understanding how to maintain this natural mental well-being and our capacity to live in the moment is what practitioners of POM generally call wisdom or maturity.

MENTAL HEALTH, TOOLKIT OF THE MIND

Mental health is our birthright. We don't have to learn how to be mentally healthy; it is built into us in the same way that our bodies know how to heal a cut or mend a broken bone. Mental health can't be learned, only reawakened. It is like the immune system of the body, which under stress or through lack of nutrition or exercise can be weakened, but which never leaves us. When we don't understand the value of mental health and we don't know how to gain access to it, mental health will remain hidden from us. Our mental health doesn't really go anywhere; like the sun behind a cloud, it can be temporarily hidden from view, but it is fully capable of being restored in an instant.

Mental health is the seed that contains self-esteem—confidence in ourselves and an ability to trust in our common sense. It allows us to have perspective on our lives—the ability to not take ourselves too seriously, to laugh at ourselves, to see the bigger picture, and to see that things will work out. It's a form of innate or unlearned optimism. Mental health allows us to view others with compassion if they are having troubles, with kindness if they are in pain, and with unconditional love no matter what they believe, how they act, or what their nationality or religion happens to be. Mental health is the source of creativity for solving problems, resolving conflict, making our surroundings more beautiful, managing our home life, or coming up with a creative business idea or invention to make our lives easier. It gives us patience for ourselves and toward others as well as patience while driving, catching a fish, working on our car, or raising a child. It allows us to see the beauty that surrounds us each moment in nature, in culture, in the flow of our daily lives.

Although mental health is the panacea for living our lives, it is nothing short of ordinary. If you reflect on your life, you will see that it has been there to direct you through all your difficult decisions. It has been available even in the most mundane of life situations to show you right from wrong, good from bad, friend from foe. Mental health has commonly been called conscience, instinct, wisdom, common sense, or the inner voice. We think of it simply as a healthy and helpful flow of intelligent thought. As you will come to see, knowing that mental health is always available and knowing to trust it allow us to slow down to the moment and live life happily.

SIX REASONS WHY IT IS CRITICAL TO SLOW DOWN TO THE SPEED OF LIFE

- Reduction of stress
- Improved physical health
- More present, intimate, and loving relationships
- Heightened sensory awareness and enjoyment of the natural beauty around us
- Greater peace of mind and serenity
- Dramatically improved ability to be productive and creative and to stay focused

UNLEASHING INNATE HUMAN POTENTIAL

Mental health is an innate capacity that is complete in itself. It is the human potential for healthy psychological functioning—self-esteem, creativity, insight, wisdom, unconditional love, healthy relationships, motivation, humor, problem solving, optimism, and many more virtues. It lies dormant in each human being in its complete form, waiting to be unleashed.

You can think of innate mental health as a one-hundred-watt lightbulb, burning constantly and consistently. The light that we see in our lives is limited by the aperture of our thinking in the moment. We may live in total darkness most of the time and have only a momentary glimpse of this light. We call this flash of light an insight, a peak experience, or a moment of happiness. As we gain more understanding of how our mind and life work, this aperture stays open farther and farther, exposing more of the light of our innate mental health. Though our mental health will fluctuate with our moods and our thoughts, the source of the light we see remains constant. As we mature, we realize more of this innate mental health in our lives. The power of this innate mental health is the unlimited human potential to live a happy and productive life.

Healthy Psychological Functioning—The Realization of Innate Mental Health

Optimism
Leadership
Passion for Life
Physical Health
Immunity to Stress
Creativity
Intimacy
Joy
Unconditional Love
Patience
Decision Making
Instinct
Vision
Adaptability
Innate Mental Health
Humor
See Beauty in Life
Perspective
Productivity
Confidence
Problem Solving
Self-Esteem
Compassion

LIVING IN THE MOMENT, ENTRY POINT
INTO HEALTHY FUNCTIONING

The entry point into healthy psychological functioning is living in the moment. But what does being in the moment really mean? We all have experienced living in the moment many times—during a crisis, being struck by the beauty of a sunset or some other natural phenomenon, falling in love, taking a shower, listening to music, hearing an inspiring speaker. During these moments, time seems to stand still and the buzz of our personal thinking briefly subsides. We see life firsthand, for we have slowed down to the speed of life. These rare moments have the ability to reduce our stress, give us hope, and fill us with joy and inspiration.

The key to making these apparently serendipitous moments the norm for our daily lives is to understand that our experience of life is directly linked to the way we are thinking. Your thought process can be either healthy or unhealthy, a topic we will discuss in great detail a little later. Knowing the difference between healthy and unhealthy thinking is one of the most important insights you can gain about your mental health.

THOUGHT, THE CREATOR OF EXPERIENCE

Thought is the power that creates human experience—the ultimate force that creates, shapes, and transforms our lives. We create our experience of life through our thinking. We can't have an experience without thought. It's as though thought is the ink in the pen of life, and we are the illustrators. What we think becomes our emotions, perceptions, sensations, decisions, behavior. It also influences the reactions we get from others and our interpretations of those reactions. Without thinking, there would be no experience. The tree may fall in the woods, but someone alive and conscious needs to experience it. We are not saying that our thinking creates the outside world in any absolute sense—the tree still falls even if we don't experience it—but our thinking does create our experience of the event.

It's impossible to experience any negative feeling without first creating a negative corresponding thought. The truth is, our thinking will *always* create the reality we perceive. For example, when we see life as being full of demands and we feel overwhelmed, our thoughts coincide with this view of life. When we are impatient, we are thinking impatient thoughts: "When is he going to call me back for that order?" When we are stressed, we are thinking stressed thoughts: "I hate my supervisor. He demands a ridiculous amount out of me. Does he think I'm Superwoman?"

These thoughts, and so many others, have the capacity to rob us of our mental health in any given moment. And because we believe that outside circumstances create our feelings, most of us try to restore our mental health from the outside in by altering those circumstances—taking a tranquilizer to relax, throwing a temper tantrum, buying another time-saving device, or quitting our job. If we believe that our feelings are determined by outside forces, it follows that we will seek something equally external in response. As we gain an understanding of our psychological experience, however, we can recognize that the actual *source* of our experience is always our thinking. Thus we can begin to restore the power in our lives.

How and what we think are the only determinants of our experience. Regardless of what happens to us—what we are going through or what circumstances we face—it is our thought process that creates our experience of that event. For example, when you are in a traffic jam, you could be thinking, "I can't believe this traffic! Why don't they build more freeways? I should move out of this city to where life is sane. I would but I can't. I'm trapped because of my mortgage and other obligations. I hate traffic!" Or you could have a totally different experience: "Boy, it's nice to just sit back and enjoy a rare, unhurried moment. I've been so busy this week. I think I'll just relax and enjoy some good music on the radio." The traffic's the same, the amount of time it takes you to get to work is exactly the same; only your experience of the event is different, and that experience is caused by your perception of it. In the second example, you've slowed down to the speed of life. It's important to know that although circumstances and difficulties vary greatly in difficulty and severity, the mental dynamic we are discussing here is always the same. In other words, although each of us will face problems far more serious than a simple traffic jam, our thinking and perception will always determine our response.

We are not saying that thought stands between us and life. We are saying that thought *is* our life. Emotion is thought. Sensation is thought. Perception is thought. Even awareness is thought. Without thought there would be no experience. Have you ever been so engaged in a task that you didn't realize you had not eaten? It's only when someone says, "Haven't you eaten yet?" that you become aware of the sensation of hunger. Or have you ever been so engrossed in a good movie or book that you completely forgot about a problem you were having? Our moment-to-moment experience is directly linked to our moment-to-moment thinking. Your problem may in fact need your attention, but you will not experience it without thinking about it.

CONSCIOUSNESS

Consciousness is the human faculty that makes thought appear real. It's the special effects department of the brain, taking any thought that comes into our mind and making it our experience of reality, in that moment, through the senses.

Consider what happens when you turn on your television. What you see on the screen is determined by what signal you are receiving. The television itself has nothing whatsoever to do with the programming. However, without a television, a signal can't be experienced.

Consciousness is like the television. It brings to the screen whatever signal the television is turned to—the murder story, the rerun, the game show, the soap opera. Whatever you are tuned in to does not originate in the television itself. The television merely transmits what's on the screen.

Like the television, consciousness brings thought (the signal) to life. Whatever we are watching comes into view through the senses (the sounds, sights, smells, tastes, and textures). As we become engrossed in the TV show, it becomes our reality.

THOUGHT + CONSCIOUSNESS = EXPERIENCE

Consciousness doesn't decide what thought to see as reality; it's much more impersonal than that. Consciousness simply serves our thinking by making it appear real. Thought and consciousness are simultaneous. For example, if you realize in the middle of your bad traffic experience that the way you are thinking is creating your upset feelings, your mind will begin to clear and a new thought will automatically replace the old perception. You may take the opportunity just to relax and enjoy the music and the time-out. Thus you will have a totally different experience—a more enjoyable one—and the time will pass more quickly. You have changed your thinking through your realization, and your experience will change accordingly.

We can't control our experience once we have created the thought. Consciousness is the passive servant of thought, automatically turning thoughts into experience. The only variable we have control over is our thinking. What is it that determines which channel we tune in to?

THOUGHT RECOGNITION

We all have the capacity to call a time-out and recognize our thinking—to see that thought is not an absolute reality but merely our experience of reality in the moment. This process of self-awareness, or thought recognition, is perhaps the most powerful tool we have to restore our mental health. When we begin to recognize that our thinking is creating our experience, we become less attached to thinking in a particular way. Then we can see that there are many channels to choose from, not just the one we are currently experiencing.

Whenever I can recognize a thought that is a negative habit—let's say it's a tendency to blame someone or get angry—I can notice myself in the act of creating a reality that is adversely affecting my state of mind. For example, I may get irritated with my co-worker for not doing what I think she should be doing. Then in the next moment I recognize that my irritation is a thought. At this moment of thought recognition, my thinking will automatically shift away from the irritation. What thought(s) occur to me next will be determined by my level of wisdom, my maturity, and my mood. We will explain this relationship in more detail later.

TWO MODES OF THOUGHT
1. The Processing/Analytical Mode

Although thought creates all experience, thought may proceed in two very different ways or modes. When you know which mode of thinking you are in, you are in a position to live in healthy psychological functioning. The first mode, the *processing mode,* resembles the way a computer processes information: storing existing data and dealing with situations that require solutions where all the variables are known.[1] We will refer to it by the terms *processing mode, process thinking, analytical thinking,* and *computer thinking.* The processing mode of thought performs the following functions:

- It stores information (memory).
- It analyzes this data (sorts it, compares it to existing information, and organizes it into beliefs, concepts, and ideas).

---

[1] Historically, Psychology of Mind practitioners have used many different sets of terms to describe the two modes of thinking ("free-flowing" thinking has also been called "diffuse," "original," the "receiver" mode, "effortless," while "process" thinking has been termed the "computer" or "analytical" mode). We believe that no single set of terms provides an all-inclusive description, so we have decided to use several sets interchangeably in the hope that different readers will find a set to which they can best relate.

- It plans our lives (creates a simulation of the future based on past memories and our imagination).
- It computes and calculates existing data in our memory in order to organize our lives and respond to situations.
- It remembers information that we have previously learned.

This analytical mode of thinking is essential to living our lives effectively. It allows us to learn everything from language to mathematics. With its help we can operate a computer, drive a car, or find our way to the grocery store without rediscovering the route every day. We can remember our name and the anniversary of our marriage (thank God for this one!), and we can do a million other tasks that, once learned, are easily repeated. The processing mode isn't the only mode we can learn in, but it is the mode most people use to learn a new habit or skill; it is the one taught in most of our schools.

The primary advantage of the processing/analytical mode is that when all the variables are known and we have all the information needed, analytical thinking is extremely fast and efficient. If, for example, I need to estimate how long it will take to get to the airport from an unfamiliar place, I can use the analytical mode to calculate distance, time, and traffic conditions.

The downside of this mode of thinking is that when we don't know all the variables, we continue to churn inside; we obsess about and rethink problems without result—a draining, frustrating, and stressful process. For example, if I don't immediately know what to do about a difficult employee situation, I might process the problem over and over again in my mind with no insight into the situation, to the detriment of other work, relationships, and my sleep. In our fast-paced world, most of us have learned to live almost exclusively in this process-oriented mode. The repeated use of process thinking when all the variables are not known, however, can and will cause stress, worry, anxiety, depression, a sense of hurry, and many other negative emotions. The improper use of this mode is also the major cause of stress that can lead to mental illness and addictions.

Much of what we learn from outside sources comes through the analytical mode. Our habits, values, skills, beliefs, attitudes, prejudices, expectations, likes and dislikes, preferences, and personality traits all are imparted through the process of conditioning and socialization. We then customize these ideas to fit particular situations through analysis and computation. This intellectual form of thinking is taught to us from birth. The processing/analytical mode of thought is highly prized in our Western culture—so highly valued that we neglect the other mode of thinking, the free-flowing mode.

2. *The Free-Flowing Mode*

The other way of thinking we have available to us operates like a river. It is always flowing, bringing us new information and thoughts in the moment—some from memory, some from the creative source. We call this mode of thinking the *free-flowing mode*. In discussing the free-flowing mode, we will interchange the terms *original thought, creative intelligence, reflective mode,* and *effortless thinking*. The primary purpose of this mode is to enjoy life, operate at peak performance and efficiency levels, and solve problems where one or more variables are unknown. In the free-flowing mode, we have the ability to think new thoughts—thoughts that we have never yet considered. People have conventionally referred to this kind of thinking as intuition, creativity, inspiration, wisdom, insight, realizations, out-of-the-blue thoughts, or divine inspiration. This mode of thinking may use memory, but when it does, it does so in a new and creative way that is relevant to the moment.

When we are in flow thinking, we experience thought as effortless. Our thinking is in the moment, responsive to whatever is happening or needed at the time. Many people wouldn't consider this mode of thought to be a form of thinking, but it most certainly is. For example, professional athletes are in the free-flowing mode when their game is on—when they are in the zone. A basketball player in the flow is shooting and passing instinctively with precise timing. A public speaker in the free-flowing mode is inspirational, creative, and responsive to the audience she is speaking to. Writers and teachers frequently refer to being "on" in their work—an effortless state of mind where appropriate thoughts continue to bubble to the surface. Children at play are in this mode frequently. The truth is, we can do almost anything in the flow mode, depending on our confidence and trust in it. Flow thinking allows us to use information that we have in our memory, but in a creative and efficient way.

When we are in the flow, thoughts seem to come to us out of the blue. Thinking takes no effort. In fact, effort will block our flow thinking and place us right back in the processing mode. Most people love it when they are in free-flowing mode, but few know how to gain access to it dependably. Many attribute flow or free-flowing thinking to circumstances—the right people, timing, magic, luck, and so forth. However, as you will see, free-flowing thinking is completely natural. This is why children spend most of their time in original thinking—it's unlearned.

In a recent survey, people were asked the question, "Where and when are you most likely to get your most creative and/or best ideas?" The three most common responses were "in the shower," "on vacation," and "driving the car." Of course, these are times when we are doing little or nothing at all, yet paradoxically we get our best thoughts and ideas at precisely these time. The reason: free-flowing thinking. It's a different type of intelligence.

It's important to know that we are *not* saying that the free-flowing mode is good and the processing mode is bad. We are saying, however, that we can learn to live in free-flowing thinking far more often than we currently do. And we can learn to use process thinking more as a tool when necessary instead of as our dominant form of thinking.

Free-flowing thinking has these advantages:

- It is stress free.
- It is nonfatiguing.
- It is ideally suited for dealing with the unknown, where creative or evolutionary thought is needed.
- It allows us to be at peak performance and enjoyment simultaneously.
- It is natural.

In addition to working with thousands of ordinary people struggling with every conceivable problem, we have worked with a number of executives who have learned the difference between analytical and free-flowing thinking. Typically, these people try to conduct a sales meeting in their free-flowing thinking mode—let's say to create a new product line. When it's time to address the nitty-gritty like budgets and logistics, however, they will consciously shift back into their processing mode. As soon as they feel they are getting bogged down or caught up in their process thinking, they will take a break, clear their mind, and get themselves back into the free-flowing mode. This helps them feel fresh, clear headed, and reenergized.

The more familiar you become with these two modes, the more natural this interplay will seem. Consider the following story, which demonstrates the interplay between the two modes of thinking. It was shared with us by Will Steger, the world-famous Arctic explorer:

In March of 1983, I was traveling between the villages of Fort Good Hope and Arctic Red River on the Mackenzie River in the Northwest Territories of Canada. I was soloing with nine dogs and was bogged down in deep snow at −60 degrees F. The Indians told me that I would find a trail, but it wasn't materializing. Slowly my food supplies started to dwindle, and I started to worry. The worry began to cost me sleep, and without sleep I started to lose energy. This was a very serious situation. I was forced to come to terms with myself to see that my thinking was starting to become a tool of self-destruction. My worry could actually kill me. I had met an Indian at Fort Good Hope whom I had respected, and he had told me many simple, wise things. He had said, "Don't worry. If you run short of food, go up to the riverbank and start a fire and get warm." He said that it was more important to rest the body and mind than to eat. These thoughts calmed me, and I became peaceful with myself and actually started to enjoy the situation. I went through my equipment in order to lighten my load and threw out everything that was nonessential, including my expensive camera gear. Being relaxed, I slept like a baby and awoke feeling fresh and excited for the new challenges of each day.

I continued for another week, breaking trail for the dogs and often hooking myself up with the dogs to pull the sled. I often traveled into the night and had to make camp in the dark at −60 degrees. As soon as I stopped, I had to light the lantern in order to light my only heat source, the stove. If I failed to light the lantern, I likely would not survive. But with a clear, relaxed mind, I looked forward to lighting the lantern. It was a logical process [proper use of analytical mode] consisting of a number of steps that depended on each other task for thinking. I remember vividly the beauty of the stars overhead. It was as if I was the sole occupant of the universe [free-flowing mode].

During the days, my thinking was quiet and I took in the beauty of my surroundings. The main danger I faced was overflow—water that flows down the mountains under the insulating layer of the snow and pools up on the ice near the riverbanks. These pools are hidden beneath the snow, and to step in one while soloing at −60 means certain death. Most of us have read Jack London's *To Build a Fire* and are familiar with what happened to the man when he accidentally stepped into some overflow. However, a very slight, almost undetectable gray color on the surface is the sign of the danger underneath. I was constantly on the watch for these signs, not by concentrating and narrowing my vision, but by being relaxed and taking in the beauty of my surroundings. In this state [free-flowing mode], overflow appeared as red flashing lights to me and I simply avoided them. Overflow appeared to me as disharmony in a world of white that surrounded me.

At one point, while I traveled on, my eyes were drawn to the distant riverbank. There was something that was out of place. It took my binoculars to identify it. It was a black dot. How could a black dot exist without being covered by four feet of snow unless it had been placed there recently? "Perhaps it was the cache of an Indian trapper," I thought. If it had recently been placed there, then there would be a trail. I halted the dogs and skied ahead to check it out. As I got closer my eyes focused entirely on the black object. It got bigger and bigger. My hopes soared. As I approached the bank I could make out a stove and some supplies. It was here that I made a major error. In my excitement of finding the cache, my mind moved out ahead of me [misuse of processing mode—future] and, unknowingly, I skied into some overflow. It felt like stepping on a down escalator when I didn't want to go down. My intuition knew and my body instantly reacted to the hydraulic feeling of the soft snow being compressed into the pool of water by my skis. I did a quick side-step shuffle with my skis. This dance kept me on the surface as I slid to a solid surface. My thinking [process] did not click in until afterward, when beads of sweat rolled down my forehead as I analyzed my mistake and I took note of it. The cache indeed marked the trail that I was looking for. I eventually made it to Arctic Red. But not before being forced to travel in a three-day storm with no food.

ACCESSING THE TWO MODES

You'll notice that these two modes of thinking function in discrete ways. You are either in one or the other. As with a walkie-talkie, you are either on "talk" or "listen"; there is nothing in between. In the processing mode it feels as if you are thinking, since processing takes concentration and effort. By releasing the button on the walkie-talkie—by clearing your mind—you automatically go into the free-flowing mode, where your thoughts flow from one to the next without effort in an intelligent though diffuse manner.

Another way to put this is to say that if you are actively thinking, you are in processing mode; if you are passively thinking, you are in the free-flowing mode. When you are in the flow, it feels as if you are not thinking at all. The thinking seems to happen through you. Free-flowing-mode thinking moves naturally, constantly bringing you fresh, harmonious thoughts. When you are in the processing mode, however, the thinking is originating from your memory.

So how do you access these two modes? We're most familiar with the processing/analytical mode only because it's the mode of thinking that we've been taught to value the most. Whenever we actually feel that we're thinking, we're in the processing mode. It can feel effortful, as if we are bearing down on a subject. It can feel stressful if we misuse it or stay in that mode too long. When we feel as if we're "in our head," we're in our processing mode. Examples of this mode include memorizing, trying to figure out directions on how to get somewhere, analyzing sales patterns, or reading directions to a new computer program. To gain access to the analytical mode, we need to remember, analyze, compute, and focus our thinking, all of which require some amount of effort.

To access the free-flowing mode we must let go of our analytical thinking. We clear the mind. Clearing the mind is much like letting the silt settle in water. You simply do nothing, and the silt automatically settles. Anything you do to try to settle the silt actually keeps it stirred up. Another way of thinking about it is to take a problem and put it on the back burner; that is, don't actively think about it, but choose to momentarily forget it so that flow thinking can go to work on it while you clean your house or putter in the garden or answer phone calls.

To gain access to original thought, we must first know that it exists, and we must value the power of it. Second, we must have faith that if we do clear the mind, this mode will automatically start feeding us a flow of thoughts—which it will. It may give us answers we weren't expecting, but they will be far superior to and wiser than thoughts we have already gone over in the mind. As we said earlier, flow thinking is better for finding an unknown solution. Process thinking can gain access only to memory data. By letting go of the analytical, trying-to-figure-it-out mode, we create a vacuum that the free-flowing mode can fill.

Not Knowing

Not knowing, that is, being willing to admit that we don't know, is one of the keys that opens the door to creative intelligence. It takes humility to open that door. Our ego doesn't like not knowing and would prefer to go over and over what we already think and believe rather than trust in a subtle, unknown process like creative intelligence. But opening ourselves to the unknown is a peaceful, productive alternative to our business-as-usual processing mode where we pretend (or hope) that we know what's going on. By clearing the mind and admitting to ourselves that we don't know, we receive answers that are often brilliant, unexpected, and just right for the situation. Recently, Richard and his wife were concerned with some health problems they were having with their youngest daughter. They had tried and tried to come up with an answer. Their efforts included several visits to specialists with no real results. Because the problem wasn't life threatening, they decided to stop trying so hard—to let go of the problem—and allow an answer to present itself. A few days later, Kris, Richard's wife, had the idea that their daughter's diet may have something to do with the problem. They had it checked out, and she was correct. Their daughter was sensitive to a certain food that she loved to eat. The problem was eliminated. No one was able to figure out what to do; instead, the process of not knowing provided an appropriate answer.

One of our clients recently talked about the value of using reflective thought:

> I was at work, trying to write a memo to another manager, and it wasn't coming out right. The memo felt hostile, sarcastic, and I knew it would backfire. Because of the negative feeling and because the process felt so difficult, I decided to put it off for a while and do some other work. Later that day, all of a sudden, it came to me exactly what I needed to say. I sat down and wrote the memo in ten minutes, and it came out great. If I had tried to write it in my processing/analytical mode, it would have backfired and it would have taken me at least an hour of writing and rewriting. Flipping to my reflective mode allowed me to prepare a very politically sensitive memo, and it didn't feel that I had to do the writing!

His willingness to let go, to not know exactly what to do, provided the answer he needed.

Free-flowing-mode thinking is essential to all personal growth, change, development, and evolution. When we learn to live in this mode most of the time and we reserve the processing mode for tasks that require planning, calculating, and analyzing, life becomes much easier and calmer. It begins to slow down. We begin to live in the deeper feelings that come with mental health—gratitude, joy, relaxation, calmness, compassion, and a sense of ease. Our thinking is responsive, that is, appropriate to the moment. We don't respond out of past habits or beliefs but instead deal with each situation in a creative, appropriate manner.

DIFFERENCES BETWEEN THE FREE-FLOWING MODE AND THE PROCESSING MODE

FREE-FLOWING MODE	PROCESSING MODE
Easy	Effortful
Passive	Active
Automatic	Contrived
Nonlinear	Linear
Deeper feelings	Conditional emotions
Uses memory selectively	Memory based and memory bound
Creative	Habitual
Spontaneous	Predictable
Big picture	Details
Forest	Trees
Vision	Tasks
Inspired	Scripted

THOUGHT RECOGNITION

Thought recognition is the key to slowing down and shifting gears. When we pause and reflect, our free-flowing mode takes over and guides us to the next step. It is our built-in automatic pilot, the wisdom that allows us to know the difference between the two modes and to know which one is called for at any given moment. When we can recognize our thinking, the next step will seem obvious—whether to put the issue on the back burner, to analyze it some more, to seek out more information, or simply to do nothing. This capacity to recognize our thoughts, with practice, becomes automatic, and our mode of thinking changes from second to second.

Consistently living in the knowledge of how our minds function is what we call healthy psychological functioning. When we are in healthy psychological functioning (or HPF), our minds work like well-tuned engines, all parts working together to move the vehicle. We know when to use the two modes of thinking, how to understand the role of our emotions, where our experience is coming from, and so on. Healthy psychological functioning is our definition of mental health. But whether or not we are in HPF depends on our level of understanding.

LEVELS OF UNDERSTANDING

Each time we have an insight into the nature of our thinking and our psychological functioning—each time we see ourselves as the thinker of our own thoughts, the creator of our moment-to-moment experience—we will experience a shift in our level of understanding. As large or small as these shifts may be, they are permanent changes, not temporary insights. And when they occur, we see life a little differently. For example, Joe remembers the first time he realized that his emotions were simply his thoughts and were not caused by other people or outside events. When this happened, he could no longer indulge in his habit of self-pity. His level of understanding had increased (he had experienced what is sometimes called a "vertical shift"), and his new level of understanding wouldn't allow him to continue in his old habit. So, for example, when he would feel rushed and hurried, rather than falling into his old habit of complaining about his schedule, he could sense his own speeded-up thinking and the role it was playing in his experience.

A client of Richard's was driving her car home after work. She was concerned about her relationship with her future husband. She was mentally reviewing many of their past arguments and rehearsing tonight's inevitable conflict. All of a sudden, something happened to her that had never occurred before. It was as if she caught herself or noticed her own thinking for the very first time. In a single instant, she realized that she spends a great deal of time in this mental rehearsal, engaging in it many times throughout the day. She thought to herself, "How can I possibly hope to have a loving relationship when I spend most of my time thinking about how awful it is?" She experienced a shift in her level of understanding. Consequently, her life is very different. Today, when negative thoughts enter her mind, she takes them far less seriously and experiences them with far more perspective. Her relationship is far more loving and stands a much better chance of staying that way.

Other self-help books and psychotherapies may teach or encourage you to change the content of your individual thoughts. What we are saying is quite different. We are saying that your thinking, your perceptions, your feelings will all change *automatically* as your level of understanding rises. As your level of understanding goes up, you will see life differently and thus you will respond differently. Generally speaking, as your level of understanding rises, you will have the experience of deeper feelings such as gratitude, calmness, peace, hope, and joy.

Imagine for a moment that your life of problems, deadlines, and difficulties is like a logjam. Trying to change each thought is like trying to pull each individual log out from the tangled mess. It would be extremely difficult, if not impossible, to do. Then imagine that you opened the dam upriver and raised the water level. The logs would all rise and break up on their own. Raising our level of understanding works in a similar way. We can open the floodgates of our mind by gaining a deeper understanding of the mind— by seeing how our own thinking contributes to our speeded-up, confused life.

A couple came to Joe for some marital counseling because of many issues: parenting philosophy differences, financial problems, sexual problems, and constant arguing. As they learned how to live in healthy psychological functioning—as their level of understanding went up—they began to see their issues in a different light. They began to see the grain of truth in each other's parenting styles. They dropped resentments about the past and began to live in feelings of warmth, love, and caring for each other. As this occurred, their sexual spark reappeared. Their arguments were replaced with heart-to-heart communication. The point is, they didn't need a class in parenting, specific sexual counseling, and communications training. Instead, these abilities became natural to them at a higher level of understanding. The shift in their level of understanding occurred at different times for each of them, but for both it occurred in a single instant—a change of heart. Their love for each other returned.

MISUSE OF THE PROCESSING MODE

When we become frightened, we tend to return to the familiar—our habits, traditions, and memories. We tend to flip into the analytical mode. We churn, process, reprocess, mull over, and relive an experience, over and over. This tendency is common to all of us, but it has never been productive. This is not what the analytical mode was meant for. Matters of the heart are generally better left to our original thought process. If we can't figure something out with analytical thinking in a few moments—or at most a few minutes—it's a good sign that we are in the wrong gear. The best strategy is to put the concern on the back burner. As we begin to sense when it's appropriate to stop using analytical thinking, the processing mode will become the servant of the free-flowing mode.

Using the processing/analytical mode for anything other than situations where all the variables are known is the wrong use of it. You can trust your feelings to alert you that you are in the wrong mode. When you are engaged in an unhealthy use of the processing mode, you will experience many negative emotions such as worry, irritation, frustration, anger, fear, resentment, jealousy, anxiety, and stress. We will discuss the role of emotions as a compass—as signals of unhealthy patterns—in the following chapter.

MISUSE OF THE FREE-FLOWING MODE

The free-flowing mode is misused much less than the processing mode in our culture. There are times however, that while we may want to be in the free-flowing mode, we may actually be better served by using the processing mode. Young children at play being called back to the classroom are a common example of this. Or we may need to plan a trip, schedule an appointment, or prepare a budget for the company. Almost always, we will want to be in the processing mode to attend to specific details. When we are learning a new task, such as mastering a computer software program or a musical instrument, we need to practice and remember the information while in the analytical mode. Just as using a calculator is quicker and makes fewer mistakes in computation than guessing the right answer, so the processing mode is better at figuring out a work schedule. At very high levels of mental health, some individuals are capable of learning new tasks in the free-flowing mode, whereas most of us tend to bounce back and forth between the two modes.

LIVING IN THE FLOW

You don't have to wait until you have a difficult problem to solve to use the free-flowing mode. If you are living your ordinary life in the flow, you will become accustomed to and proficient at it, and you will build up an immunity to getting caught up in your negative habits of thought when trouble does arrive. It might be a good idea, for example, on a day when you are in a good mood, but your mind is restless, to observe that if you don't give in to the habit of feeding your mind with excessive thoughts, even though they may seem positive and harmless, you will stay in the free-flowing mode for longer periods of time.

Even as insights come to you, see if you can avoid the habit of thinking about them too much. Let that creative thought continue to flow down the river instead of plucking it out for analytical inspection. You can trust that the insight will still be there when you need it. You can resist the temptation to hang onto it by memorizing it and taking it apart piece by piece. Learning to operate on a moment-to-moment basis with a quiet mind builds up a reserve of healthy functioning that helps you live in it when the going gets tough. Living in the flow becomes a familiar way of life.

SLOWING DOWN TO THE MOMENT

In this chapter we have demonstrated the possibility as well as the practicality of living in the moment. Slowing down to the speed of life is not just possible; it is the way we were meant to live. In summary:

1. We talked about innate mental health as the potential of all human beings to live in healthy psychological functioning. This mental health is a toolkit for living. We have within us the capacity for self-esteem, unconditional love, wisdom, humor, compassion for others, creativity, joy, and an intelligent form of thought that guides each step of our journey in life.
2. We learned that the entry point into this mental health is living in the moment. In order to understand how to live in the moment, we need to understand how we create our psychological experience of life. We learned that all experience comes from our thinking and that thinking, when combined with consciousness, gives us the experience of our reality. Our behavior and the consequences we receive in life are a direct result of this process.
3. We learned that there are two distinct modes of thought. These two types of thought are known as the processing/analytical mode and the free-flowing/reflective mode.
4. We learned that the purpose of the processing mode is to deal with situations in which all the variables are known.
5. We learned that free-flowing mode is for dealing with the

unknown, with change and evolution. It is relying on
insight instead of solely on memory. It is also the mode
that allows us to enjoy life to its fullest. We then discussed how to access the two modes of thinking and the
pros and cons of each.

6. We also learned that the primary purpose of learning
   these principles is to raise our level of understanding. As
   our understanding increases, we gain insights into life,
   and with them our thinking, feelings, and perceptions
   change automatically. There's very little that we have
   to do.

7. Last, we found that healthy psychological functioning is
   a process that is natural to all of us. As we recognize
   our unhealthy thinking, we return to our default setting—healthy psychological functioning. When we
   function with mental health, we know how and when
   to use the two modes, we understand the role of our
   emotions as a compass, and we experience increased
   thought recognition.

In the next chapter, we will go into the nuts and bolts of
navigating our thinking, moods, and emotions. This will give
you a practical understanding of living in the moment.

CHAPTER 2

Navigating Your Thinking

If you think of your life as a journey and yourself as the captain of your ship, you know that nothing is more important to your survival and the quality of your life than learning to navigate efficiently. Most of us, however, have picked up mental habits that interfere with our ability to stay on course, change direction, slow down, or gain access to our wisdom. Instead of going with the flow of our journey by using appropriate and effortless motion, most of us resist and struggle with each wave, turning what could be a peaceful ride into difficult, often painful experiences.

As you look around at the people in your life, you'll observe that most of us had poor training in the use of our navigational skills. Rarely have we been taught that different circumstances in life are best suited for different modes of

thinking or that our analytical thinking can (and does) interfere with—even sabotage—the quality of our lives. Because
we rely so heavily on our processing thought, we often roll
up our sleeves and get to work (speeding up) when we would
be better served by slowing down or backing off. We try to
force answers instead of allowing them to unfold, and we try
to think our way to solutions that would come easily to a
quiet, receptive mind. As a result, we end up rushing around
confused, frustrated, and frantic. This speeded-up way of living is reinforced by the hurried, frenetic pace of our modern
technological culture. Because most other people are also living in a hurried state of mind, we mindlessly accept a frantic
pace as inevitable, but it's not.

Learning to gain access to this quieter mode of thinking
involves recognizing how important and practical it is. This is
particularly true when we need original answers to heartfelt
issues, when we are confronted with a difficult moment, when
we need to be at peak performance levels, or when we want to
slow down our overactive mind or the pace of our life.

Most of us wouldn't dream of using a computer to solve a
marriage or parenting problem or to ask the boss for a raise;
these issues require creativity and insight. But in essence,
that's what we do when we rely too heavily on our analytical
thinking in an attempt to find answers to these types of
issues. New solutions don't come from the processing mode
of thinking. Rather, the answers we need come from a change
of heart, from seeing life differently—from the flow. They
come from the unknown, the territory of flow thinking. Not
knowing is one of the key ways to gain access to the reflective
mode. When we admit we don't know and are confident that
an answer will come, we will soon begin to see that the free-

flowing mode will serve us up the answer that we need. The same is true with many difficult moments in day-to-day living. If we try to think through what we are confronted with—if we try to make sense of our moments with our analytical thinking instead of allowing our free-flowing mode thinking to intervene—we will often end up frustrated and anxious.

You'll begin to notice (if you haven't already) that whenever you feel rushed, speeded up, or out of control, you will have navigated away from healthy psychological functioning and into the realm of an overactive mind. In these instances, a moment of recognition can usually bring you back to the present moment and slow you down to a more optimal level of functioning. Remember, however, that there is nothing wrong with analytical thinking. The goal is not to stop thinking or to make analytical thinking your enemy. Often your analytical mind will serve you in healthy, necessary ways, as we have discussed. The key is to become aware when your thinking is serving you and when it's taking you away from where you want to be.

For example, Richard remembers a time when he was calculating the approximate number of chairs he would need for a public lecture he was going to give. The hotel he was speaking at had called to inform him that they needed to know within a few hours. Clearly, Richard needed to use his analytical thinking to determine the approximate number of guests that would be attending. Unfortunately, in this particular instance, he allowed his analytical thinking to continue long after it had served its purpose. He began to think thoughts like, "What if no one comes? What if I tell the hotel I need lots of chairs and not very many people show up? It would be so embarrassing. I wish I were more organized. Why do I allow myself to get into these messes?" On and on he went, having a full-blown thought attack for at least five minutes before having thought recognition and realizing what was happening. As soon as this occurred, his thinking began to slow down. What he needed to be doing—instead of using his thinking to frighten himself—was to be in his reflective mode, not processing mode, so that he could reflect on his talk that evening. Had he continued on much further in an inappropriate use of his thinking, it could very well have affected his talk later that day.

Most of us have learned to accept our poor mental navigational skills as the norm without realizing that we do, in fact, have options. We don't realize that the root of being angry, hurried, or stressed is a mind that has lost sight of its healthy psychological functioning, a mind too dependent on analytical thinking. When that same mind slows down to the speed of life and begins to recognize thought for what it is, its inherent wisdom will flow. The same issues will appear in an entirely new light.

You can learn to reach your free-flowing mode of thinking—the quiet and peaceful mode of thinking—by simply knowing and trusting that it exists. The first step is recognizing the mode of thought you are currently using by letting your feelings be your guide.

THE RELATIONSHIP BETWEEN THOUGHT AND FEELING

Every negative feeling we experience is a thought. As a matter of fact, feelings are thoughts in a more subtle form.

You experience thoughts in the form of feelings and sensations. For example, it's impossible to feel angry without having angry thoughts or to feel stressed without having stressful thoughts. If you need to verify this, we encourage you to try a little experiment that we have used with clients for years.

REFLECTION

Imagine, for a moment, that your goal was to feel as angry as possible. How would you go about it? Very simply, you'd have to think about something that makes you particularly angry in order to feel angry feelings. Otherwise, you'd be unable to recreate the feelings. Try this right now and you'll see what we mean.

Thinking and feelings are inseparable. You think, you feel. You may not always be aware of the thoughts you are thinking or even that you are thinking at all. Take a look at this typical exchange with a client:

Client: I feel very stressed out. My life is too complicated.

Richard or Joe: Do you recognize that you were having stressful thoughts?

Client: I didn't have any stressful thoughts; I just feel stressed. It's my life that's causing my stress. That's why I'm here!

This client's take on his stress is hardly unusual. While this person might not dream of spending hours obsessing about a single frustrating thought, he might be thinking dozens of fleeting stressful thoughts and rarely, if ever, be aware that he is doing so. In other words, he has no thought recognition. This habit feels normal to him and, therefore, is invisible to his awareness. This client has no idea that his thoughts and the way he is seeing his life are contributing to his feelings of stress. He assumes that his feelings are simply the result of his stressful life circumstances.

Thinking about something can occur over a period of time, or it can take only a second. In either case, there is a direct relationship between your thoughts and the way you feel. If you have the thought, even in passing, that "Tomorrow is going to be difficult," it's no coincidence that you are now feeling a little worried. Your mind isn't in the moment; it's on tomorrow. Similarly, if you have the thought, "My life is a mess; nothing ever goes right," the fact that you are feeling sorry for yourself is not a surprise. The feeling arrived the instant the thought came to mind. If, instead, you had been thinking, "Gosh, there is a lot of work to be done around here. I wonder if other people feel the same way," your feelings would have been quite different—less antagonistic, perhaps.

FEELINGS: YOUR NAVIGATIONAL COMPASS

We'd like you to consider a new way of thinking about your feelings that will greatly simplify your ability to navigate toward your healthy psychological functioning.

When you get right down to it, there are really only two types of feelings: comfortable and uncomfortable. There are feelings that you like and others that you don't, feelings that are nourishing and others that are painful. The way most people think of their feelings is to label and sort them into very specific categories—angry, afraid, happy, jealous, stressed out, peaceful, rushed, and so forth—but the fact remains, some of these feelings are comfortable, others are not.

Your feelings are a navigational tool that can help guide you toward healthy psychological functioning. They let you know which mode of thinking you are in. Generally speaking, if you're feeling comfortable it suggests that you are in a healthy mode of thinking. If, however, you are feeling uncomfortable, it suggests that you are caught up, to one degree or another, in some form of unhealthy thinking. In these instances, it may be time to back off and reflect. In the free-flowing mode of thinking you may experience an uncomfortable feeling, but it just flows along. In the processing mode you tend to dam it up and analyze it.

Your comfortable feelings can be thought of as ideal room temperature. When you are experiencing ideal room temperature, no mental adjustment needs to be made. In all likelihood, you're using thinking that is appropriate to the task at hand. But just as a thermostat alerts the furnace when it's time to kick on, your feelings alert you when you need a mental adjustment of some kind. We are not suggesting that comfortable feelings are always good and that uncomfortable feelings are always bad. What we are saying is that when you are experiencing uncomfortable feelings, or if you're feeling rushed or speeded up, just recognize these feelings and don't process where they came from. You certainly don't need to beat yourself up or become judgmental. Perhaps the best thing to do is to simply observe what is going on. In time, this simple observation will take you back to free-flowing thinking.

Let us share with you a personal example of how this dynamic works in day-to-day life. The other day Richard was at the grocery store when two punk-rocker teenagers walked by him. They had spiked hair, dirty clothing, and dozens of tattoos on their bodies. They were listening to loud music inside the store.

A few minutes later Richard realized that he was feeling uncomfortable. Something was off. The awareness of these uncomfortable feelings was followed by a realization that he had been thinking very judgmentally about the two teens. Like a lightbulb going on in his mind, the simple act of recognizing his uncomfortable feelings—that something was off—reminded him that a shift in his thinking was in order. Richard's assumption that uncomfortable feelings are always a sign of dysfunctional thinking put this experience in a different light. Almost instantly, his judgmental thoughts vanished and were replaced by thoughts of compassion. He realized that it wasn't his place to judge other people.

Uncomfortable feelings are a tip-off—a warning, an alert that you're off track—thinking dysfunctionally. This doesn't mean "bad"; in fact, in this sense, uncomfortable feelings are your friend!

Just as the warning lights on the dashboard of your car alert you to potential danger, your negative feelings alert you that your thinking is no longer serving you. Without your feelings to alert you that a problem is lurking, you'd have no way to determine when you have drifted off course.

If you constantly label your negative feelings—for example, "I'm angry"—instead of simply noticing "I'm uncomfortable," you keep the negative feeling alive in your thinking, increasing the degree to which you are caught up and concerned about how you are feeling. Your thinking becomes a spiral whereby the more analytical you become about how you are feeling, the more trapped you will become.

The act of noticing uncomfortable feelings—seeing them as a warning flag—reminds you that you are thinking; it wakes you up. This simple act clears your mind and points you back in the direction of your healthy thought process. Let us share one more personal example to reinforce this important point:

Richard's seven-year-old daughter has recently gotten into the habit of procrastinating while getting ready for school. A few days ago Richard received a phone call fifteen minutes before it was time to take her to school. Before taking the call, he gently and respectfully asked his daughter if she would be sure she was ready to go by the time he finished this call. She assured him in no uncertain terms that she would. It was particularly important on this day that she cooperate because Richard had an important meeting to attend only minutes after dropping her off.

Richard had to end his phone conversation early, telling the person he was speaking to, "I must go now. I've got to take my daughter to school." He called his daughter, only to discover that she hadn't even started to get ready. He experienced an immediate shift in the way he was feeling. He was angry, disappointed, and worried about being late to his meeting. It all happened in an instant.

Luckily, Richard has come to understand his feelings as a signal that his thinking is about to get himself into trouble—a sign that he's drifting into unhealthy thinking. In this instance, his feelings alerted him that he was off balance and reactive. Rather than immobilizing him, his uncomfortable feelings were a blessing in disguise. They woke him up and allowed a shift to take place in his thinking. The practice of thought recognition immediately cleared his mind and his thinking, which made him less reactive and brought him back to flow thinking. In a sense, flow thinking is like a self-correcting mechanism. The act of thought recognition does all the work.

This more responsive type of thinking helped Richard regain his perspective and decide what to do next. Because he was able to retrieve his bearings, he didn't waste much time fretting about what had happened (something he would have surely done a few years ago). Instead of wasting time, he used the energy of being present in the moment to help his daughter get ready for school.

In no way are we suggesting that Richard didn't get angry and frustrated—he did. But he wasn't immobilized by these feelings. He didn't see his uncomfortable feelings as something to fear or react against but rather as information that guided him in a different direction. Instead of processing the content of his angry feelings, he used them as a navigational instrument to steer toward flow thinking. Clearly, his daughter did neglect to follow his instructions, and he did have a heart-to-heart talk with her about this problem later that evening. He knew that he had to get a meeting of the minds with her about what was expected of her in the mornings. We point this out because it's important to know that backing off your forceful thinking doesn't mean you pretend that things don't bother you or that you don't need to respond. The truth is, you'll respond *more* appropriately and with *greater* wisdom and effectiveness if you learn to trust your flow thinking and act from your healthy psychological functioning. Rather than reacting to life, you'll begin to respond to life with greater perspective.

Learning to respond to adversity in this new way begins by understanding your feelings in a different light—not as something to fear, repress, avoid, or express, but simply as a navigational compass. They offer you an opportunity to realize that your thinking is dysfunctional so that you will move to a different mode. If you wake up and have that understanding, you will automatically, effortlessly, go into a different mode. Part of coming to that understanding is simply learning to recognize when you have a negative thought. Then, all of a sudden, your understanding takes over and leads you into a different mode. No mental process is necessary; it happens all by itself.

THOUGHT RECOGNITION REVISITED

The negative effects of thought arise when we lose sight of thought recognition—when we forget that we are thinking and that our thinking is creating our experience. The key is to remember that thought isn't something that happens to us; it is something we are doing on a moment-to-moment basis, whether we realize it or not. It's easy to forget that we are thinking. When we do forget, we blame our circumstances for our unhappiness and frustration, and our mind spins, often wildly out of control. This is a major factor in our almost constant feeling of being in a hurry. An important point, however, is that thought recognition does not necessarily mean that you see yourself creating thoughts; it's just a recognition that you must be thinking because you're having thoughts.

While most of us wouldn't write ourselves a nasty letter, read it, and then feel offended, this is precisely what we do with regard to our thinking. We might take seriously a string of thoughts about how life isn't fair, then wonder why life never seems fair. Or we might fill the mind with thoughts about our never-ending list of things to do and simultaneously wonder why we constantly feel rushed, as if there isn't enough time. The solution to these and other types of frustrations is to begin to establish the connection between our thinking and the way we feel. When we remember that we are the thinker and that it is our thoughts about life that determine how we feel, it allows us to step back, slow down the speed of life, and regain perspective. We can then observe rather than dive into our thinking, which gives us new options for relating to our circumstances and the pace of our lives.

It can be difficult to remember that thoughts are the product of our own thinking. We lose sight of this capability, unlike other capabilities we know we have. It's easy, for example, to remember that our voices are the product of our ability to speak. That's why it's almost impossible to scare yourself with your own voice. You can scream all you want, but you still won't be able to frighten yourself! You simply are too aware that the sound you are hearing is being created by you. It is interesting to note that young infants will scare themselves with their own crying until the moment that they realize it is their crying that is producing the noise.

Thinking, however, is very different. Because thinking goes on automatically, it's much closer to us. Because we're always doing it, it's easy to forget that it's happening, and it becomes invisible. That's why thoughts become our reality.

The result is that when a thought pops into our head, instead of saying to ourselves, "There's another one," we react to it as if it were outside ourselves. We take the thought seriously and become concerned and reactive.

As our level of understanding rises, we begin to realize earlier and earlier that we are thinking—and we can recognize more of the negative and insecure thoughts that enter the mind. By paying less attention to our own negativity, our head clears and elicits our healthy thought process. As our level of understanding goes up, we can relate to our thinking in a new way by noticing and observing our thoughts without being overly attached to their content. Our thinking becomes more visible to us.

OUR THINKING CAN TRICK US

Let's consider the following example of how thought can be misunderstood and how this lack of understanding can affect you. Suppose your car breaks down and you manage to pull off the road onto the shoulder. While you're looking under your hood without a clue as to what to do next, you hear two people in a pickup truck calling out to you as they drive away. You can't quite make out what they are saying, but you imagine you hear the words, "Too bad, sucker." You respond with disgust and anger. "What's the matter with those jerks," you think. "I hope they have an accident." Your rapid-fire thoughts make you even more frustrated than before and end up ruining your entire afternoon. Hours later, you remain angry, well after the tow truck has taken you to a garage. Every few minutes you remember the jerks, and as you think about them, you become angry and reactive. When you get to work, you snap at your boss, who merely expressed concern when you were late.

Here's the catch to this example: You misunderstood the men in the pickup. They really said, "We'll call a tow truck." They not only had no bad intentions toward you; they drove fifteen minutes out of their way to find a telephone!

Unfortunately, all of us have experienced this type of misunderstanding many times. In fact, in less dramatic fashion, we have similar experiences many times a day. We lose recognition that we are thinking. We fill our heads with information, which we then interpret as reality instead of remembering that it's just thought. It's always our own thinking that actually upsets us. If, in this example, you had recognized that it was your own thinking, not the malice of two strangers, that was so upsetting, you could have dismissed the thoughts and quickly put the event behind you.

A critical point to keep in mind is that even if the two men in the pickup had yelled, "Too bad, sucker," it still would have been your thoughts about the incident, not the incident itself, that elicited negative feelings. With this thought recognition, you still would have been able to let go of the incident and go on with your day.

MOODS

When you're in a good mood, life seems good and appears to flow. You have perspective, wisdom, and common sense. There seems to be enough time. Your problems seem less formidable and easier to solve. If you need to take action, you do so. You feel grateful for your relationships, and you don't take things personally. You take differences in stride and appreciate the time you have with those you love. Life seems almost like a dance—you feel graceful. There is very little struggle in higher moods.

In lower or bad moods, life looks serious and hard. There never seems to be enough time. You often feel rushed. Not only do you forget to stop and smell the roses; you don't even see them. You are always in a hurry, one step behind. You take things personally and react to adversity rather than responding to it with perspective. You're uptight and defensive. You can't enjoy yourself in a low mood because your mind is focused on the negative.

Remember, however, that this description of moods is very general. In reality, every person has a different experience of moods. For some people a high mood is just feeling a sense of relief from their problems and a low mood is feeling horrified, whereas for other people a low mood is feeling slightly stressed and a high mood is feeling euphoric. The point is that we feel better in high moods than we do in lower moods. What are your mood shifts like?

Mood shifts can be subtle. You can easily miss them, missing also the way changing moods alter your perceptions. How many times have you left home in the morning smiling, feeling grateful for your job, and by noon you're complaining about the job, thinking of quitting? One day you're feeling love toward your spouse, and the next day you're considering divorce. Or one day you love being a parent, and the next you wish you'd never had children. What has really changed in a mood shift? It is only the quality of our thinking.

Such quick and complete contrasts may seem strange and even comical, but we're all like this. In higher moods, life seems precious. In low moods, we lose our perspective and life seems grim. It's critical to remember that it's not our lives that change so drastically but rather our moods and the accompanying feelings that shape our perception of life.

While you certainly can't avoid low moods—they are part of being human—you can learn to understand them and take them less seriously. Moods are simply fluctuations in the quality of our thinking. They are like internal weather. Bad moods are simply a flurry of negative thoughts. The same surroundings fill our world; they just appear different in different lighting and conditions—different thoughts and perceptions. Although we know moods are connected to our thinking, we don't know what causes these fluctuations, but it doesn't really matter once we learn how to deal with them. Rather than believing that we are seeing life realistically, we can learn to question our judgment when we're feeling off. Instead of looking for validation of how horrible life has suddenly become, we can recognize a mood shift and say, "Of course I'm seeing life this way. I'm always pessimistic when I'm feeling down—it's just my thinking."

The trick is to learn to be grateful for high moods and graceful in low moods. Despite the common tendency to analyze our lives when we are in a low mood, our best option is actually to do nothing; simply acknowledge the mood, don't take it too seriously, and let it pass. You may find that this is just the opposite of what most of us do in low moods. More often than not, we try to think our way out of them. We struggle and use force. But we can't think our way out of a low mood because, as we have seen, our thinking feeds our feelings. The more we think analytically in a low mood, the worse we feel.

Overreacting to low moods is understandable because low moods feel so bad and make our lives appear serious and urgent. In fact, this sense of urgency is the reason we tend to start our most serious discussions while we are feeling down. We try to solve our problems, figure out what's wrong with us and others, make major decisions—all when we are low and have lost sight of our wisdom and common sense. The simple act of acknowledging a low state of mind—knowing we are seeing life in a distorted way and distrusting our thinking in these lower states—can help open the door to healthy psychological functioning. Urgent issues and problems will always seem less pressing and easier to address when our mood has a chance to rise.

When we stop feeding our low moods with analytical thinking, it helps us to slow down. We begin to realize that if we have a legitimate problem that needs attending to, it most certainly will still be there when our mood rises and our wisdom holds sway.

GETTING CAUGHT IN THE MOMENT

We have described the key to our mental health as being present in the moment. The obstacle to experiencing the present moment is being caught up in analytical thinking—mulling over the same thoughts again and again and not recognizing the pattern. Being caught up means obsessing over things, having a great deal on your mind, and not recognizing that you are temporarily in a low mood.

We can (and do) get caught up about practically anything—the height of our neighbors' fence, our financial situation, the mean look we received from a stranger, the length of the grocery line, our employer's unrealistic expectations, our spouse's spending habits, and so forth. Anything and everything is fair game when it comes to being caught up.

One of the most important ideas to understand in order to slow down to the speed of life is this: The fact that you're caught up in your thinking is more relevant to the way you feel than to the specific details of whatever you're caught up about!

This doesn't mean that what you're concerned about isn't sometimes important. If it truly is, you're going to want to do something about it. Alcoholics need to stop drinking. Unemployed workers need to find jobs. Single parents with five children need to find ways to manage their responsibilities. Politicians and elected officials need to find solutions to societal problems. The question isn't whether or not we're going to do something about our concerns, but rather how we're going to go about it—whether we'll do it from a healthy flow of thought or from a frenetic, troubled state of mind.

Given that thoughts and feelings are one and the same, the more caught up you are, the worse you're going to feel. No one, from janitors in department stores to CEOs of giant companies, has yet said, "I'm better off when I'm caught up than when I'm calm and relaxed." The fact is, when you feel overwhelmed by your thinking, you aren't at your best— ever. Among other things, you lose your ability to see the bigger picture. You imagine your problems and concerns to be bigger than they actually are, and you see no viable solutions. You rush around, yet you accomplish very little. You lose sight of your healthy psychological functioning.

When you are caught up, you are somewhere other than the present moment. Your mind is reviewing your past, actively thinking about something that is over—whether it's an event from your childhood or something that happened at the breakfast table this morning. Or your mind is rehearsing something that may or may not happen in the future—what it's going to be like when your children leave home, what your wife will think when you tell her you accepted a job in another state, and so on. As a result, you're not right here, right now, in the moment. In no way are we trivializing your concerns. Instead, we are suggesting that thinking is what's pulling you away from the moment and away from your healthy psychological functioning.

FORKS IN THE ROAD

At each moment of life, you are at a fork in the road, and you will choose which direction to take. We'll call the road branching off to the left "Caught Up Avenue." This is the route you follow when you start analyzing what's going on, imputing motives to people's actions, or imagining what they are thinking—an unhealthy processing mode. This is a familiar direction because we take it many, many times a day.

Here's an example of a trip down Caught Up Avenue. Sarah wakes up Monday morning and begins her routine. It's a beautiful day outside, and she's just had a nice weekend. She's looking forward to next weekend when she and some friends are going camping. All of a sudden, Sarah looks at the clock and it's 7:15 A.M. A series of thoughts pops into her head: "Damn, I'm going to have to hurry again. The traffic has gotten so bad. I hate Mondays. God, I have a lot to do. Oh, no, I've got that meeting with Joe, and I forgot to send him the plans last week." Does this sound familiar? It should, because it's a typical way many people start the day.

Sarah is in an early stage of being caught up in her thinking. It starts out rather harmlessly, and because it seems so normal it's almost certainly invisible. Sarah has no idea that she is caught up, nor does she care. She is unaware that being caught up affects her sense of well-being, her wisdom, and her ability to solve the minor problems that have come to mind. To her, it simply appears as though her life is too complicated and stressful. It never occurs to her that her thinking is playing a role in her feelings of overwhelm and stress, much less that it is the cause. You can imagine how her day will unfold if she continues in this direction, which, in all likelihood, is precisely what she will do.

Without recognition of what she is doing to herself, she will simply continue to think in the same way. She will think of additional things she has to do until she's feeling completely overwhelmed. She will probably discuss her feelings of overwhelm with her friends at work and will mentally rehearse many of her upcoming work-related responsibilities. She will feel tired, resentful, angry, and burned out, probably before noon. But, again, to her, it's "just the way things are." It's the nature of her job. It's the job's fault. She believes that if she had a different job, she wouldn't feel so stressed out.

You can probably see, however, that this isn't true. Sarah's mental tendency to stay away from the present moment—to take her thoughts far too seriously—is all too familiar. Although the details would be different, the identical process would repeat itself whether her job were waiting on tables, running a giant company, or teaching school. It makes no difference what your life looks like from the outside; it's how you relate to your thinking that matters most. How we relate

to our thinking is totally dependent on our level of understanding—on how we see life.

Keep in mind, too, that in this example we are using a
person whose life is not particularly difficult. Imagine what
would happen if Sarah were unemployed, living in public
housing, or addicted to cocaine. What would happen to her if
her husband were to leave her and take away their children?
The same process would exist in her thinking, only the stakes
would be much higher.

Now, let's look a the same scenario but with a different outcome. This time, Sarah sees the other fork in the road. The
road to the right represents her healthy psychological functioning. We'll call this direction "Serenity Lane." Sarah wakes up
Monday morning and begins her routine. It's a beautiful day
outside, and she's just had a nice weekend. She's looking forward to next weekend when she and some friends are going
camping. All of a sudden, Sarah looks at the clock and it's 7:15
A.M. A series of thoughts pops into her head: "Damn, I'm going
to have to hurry again. The traffic has gotten so bad. I hate
Mondays. God, I have a lot to do. Oh, no, I've got that meeting
with Joe, and I forgot to send him the plans last week."

This time, however, Sarah notices what's happening to
her thinking. Her uncomfortable feelings alerted her that
something was off. She catches herself getting caught up. She
says to herself, "Wow, there I go again," as she notices her
mind drifting away from the present moment and filling up
with concerns and resentments.

Sarah can see how easy and seductive it would be to follow her negative trains of thought. But she realizes that,
tempting as it may be, getting caught up in her thinking, not
what she's caught up about, is the problem. She knows that

her unhealthy process thinking is the cause of her current feelings of stress and that she would be equally immobilized if, instead of being caught up about her hurried life, she were immersed in worries about making her car payment. Knowing her feelings are her thoughts frees her to respond to life in a healthier way.

Because she recognized herself early and came back to free-flowing thinking, she could regain her emotional bearings quickly and navigate toward healthy psychological functioning. She was able to chuckle at herself for falling into a familiar habit. Instead of allowing her mind to spin out of control and ruin her day, she was able to slow down to the speed of life and enjoy the time she had left at home before leaving for work.

Sarah is well aware that she forgot to give Joe the plans. Because her mind has slowed down, however, she is less distracted by her frantic thoughts, and a strategy pops into her head about the best way to deal with the problem. She doesn't pretend that she isn't busy, and she does plan to attend to each of her responsibilities. Her schedule and list of things to do is still full, yet because her mind is in the moment rather than focused on so many future moments and concerns, her list appears much more manageable. She calmly decides that she will carefully set priorities and do one thing at time to the best of her ability. Even more important, she sees that nothing on her list (or on any list) is worth ruining her life over.

As our level of understanding rises, we begin to recognize our thinking more and more in the moment. It occurs to us more frequently that we are thinking—either in free-flowing or processing mode. Recognizing that we are thinking has the effect of freeing us from mental habits that have kept us from healthy psychological functioning and that keep us in a constant rush. In a sense, what we need to know is what not to do. When you remove weeds from an otherwise beautiful garden, what you are left with is pure beauty. You didn't have to add more plants, you only took away what was interfering with the beauty already there. Similarly, when you remove unhealthy thinking, you are left with healthy psychological functioning. Pure and simple. As we notice our thinking that is removed from the present moment, we shift out of the processing mode and into free-flowing mode. Our mental health emerges, and we begin to slow down to the speed of life.

SUMMARY

When we slow down to the speed of life, we tap into a peaceful feeling that permeates our entire being and way of life. Rather than constantly feeling rushed, hurried, and frustrated, we feel calm, joyful, and curious. Bad things still happen when we slow down, but they never look as bad as when we're speeded up.

The metaphor of the baseball player is helpful to illustrate this point. When a major league batter is "on" his game, when he feels "in the zone," the pitched ball appears to be coming at him in slow motion. In actuality, of course, the ball is zooming toward him, often at speeds of over a hundred miles per hour! The facts don't change. What changes is his perception, which in turn increases his confidence in his ability. To him the ball looks like it is going slower, so hitting the ball seems easy in the free-flowing mode.

The same process happens in our ordinary lives. As the mind slows down, we are able to see life much more clearly.

We have many of the same issues to contend with, but they look different. Rather than appearing to be emergencies that are smothering us, they look like issues that need resolving or opportunities in disguise.

Feelings are a mechanism to let us know when our minds are operating too quickly and when it's time to slow down. Just as a timer goes off to signal that dinner is ready, an internal buzzer goes off when you are thinking in an unhealthy way. If you listen to these feelings and trust what they are trying to tell you, you will begin to experience the peace and joy of your mental health. Never again will life seem like such an emergency!

———◆———

CHAPTER 3

Getting Back to the Moment

The present is the moment,
the past was a moment,
the future will be a new moment.

Unfortunately, it often seems that just about the time life is going smoothly, we find some way to get caught up, once again, in our unhealthy thinking—speeded up, worrying about a bill, concerned about the future, regretting the past, resenting something that happened at work, or simply consumed in our to-do list for tomorrow. There are an infinite number of ways to get off track. However, they all have one thing in common: They are the result of our own thinking. When we recognize that we are thinking, however—when we remember that *we* are the thinker responsible for the feelings we are experiencing—we then have the capacity to wake up and bring ourselves gently back to the moment.

In this chapter we will describe a few ways to get back on track, quicker and easier—when you lose it or when you are speeded up. You may want to refer back to these points when you feel yourself speeding up or moving too quickly. Four simple keys help you get back to the moment.

FOUR KEYS TO GETTING BACK TO THE MOMENT

1. Listening
2. Seeing the wisdom in not knowing
3. Having faith in the free-flowing mode
4. Putting your problems on the back burner

1. LISTENING

Very few of us actually listen to others. Instead, while someone else is talking we are usually absorbed in our own personal world of process thinking, at best respectful as we simply wait for our turn to speak. Listening, however—true and sincere listening—is one of the main mechanisms to bringing our attention back to the moment, back to healthy psychological functioning.

Most of us have been indoctrinated through our educational system to listen almost exclusively with our analytical, process-oriented mode thinking, which consists of concentrating and memorizing. We mentally compare what we are listening to with what is already familiar to us—agreeing, disagreeing, and processing the data as it enters our mind. Although this type of listening can be appropriate for some learning, there are times when this form of listening tends to take us away from the moment.

The type of listening we are suggesting here is different. It's listening with nothing on our minds—no interpretation, prejudice, preconception, expectation, or anticipation. This type of listening takes place in the free-flowing mode of thought. When we are listening in this way, our thoughts flow gently, and we have the capacity to become touched by life as it is being created in each moment—one instant after another. When we are listening in this manner, we can easily notice when we stray off track, out of the moment.

Consider what happens when you are listening to music purely for enjoyment. You aren't listening to criticize the melody, memorize the lyrics, or figure out what key it is being played in; you are simply enjoying the music. When you listen to music this way, you *feel* the music, and it touches you.

If you listened to the identical music from your analytical mode of thinking, you might be able to describe the particulars of the lyrics, the beat, the melody, and so on. Chances are, however, you would not be moved or touched by the music.

When we go through life as a "soft listener," we stay awake to our thinking, meaning that we are constantly aware of the fact that we are thinking as well as of the effect that our thinking has on us. We fully experience our feelings and sensations, which allows us to navigate smoothly through the moods, emotions, and circumstances of life.

It's helpful to be aware of the types of thinking that take us out of the moment—away from the here and now. They are *interpreting* and *agreeing/disagreeing*.

1. *Interpreting*. When we interpret what someone is saying or something we are observing, we are filtering the

experience through our memory. When we do this, we are, in a sense, reexperiencing our past instead of experiencing the moment as it arises. If we are busy interpreting what we are hearing as we are listening, we will be determining what we like and dislike based entirely on how it fits into our existing belief structure—what we already like and dislike and what we already assume to be true—rather than experiencing it in its own right. For example, suppose your spouse is speaking to you about a disagreement she had with your next-door neighbor. If you are interpreting what you are hearing as she is speaking, you will be drawing conclusions in your mind even before she is finished. You might be thinking, "I've heard this before," or "She's always arguing with someone," or "That neighbor sure is difficult." Your experience of the moment will be contaminated and affected by your assumptions and memories of the past. It is this type of listening that leads people to say things like, "He never listens to me." While you may be physically present, you aren't listening fully in the moment. True listening is being open to something new without interpreting it through our past conditioning or being overly affected by our own thoughts of the event. In this example it would be receiving your spouse's comments without your own inner commentary. You would be receiving her words with love and respect—the type of listening that leads someone to say, "He really listens well."

2. *Agreeing/Disagreeing.* The second type of listening that takes us away from the moment might be called agree-or-disagree listening. When we listen to something while simultaneously thinking about whether we agree or disagree with it, we severely limit what we can learn. It's as if we are trapped within our existing beliefs. You probably have spo-

ken to someone who offered a running commentary on your words: "That's right, I know. No, that's not right. Yeah. No. Right on. I don't think so." Nearly everything you said passed through the other person's filter of agreement or disagreement. Again, as with interpreting, agree-or-disagree thinking is filtering the present conversation through past beliefs; it is not really listening.

If we listen with a quiet, open mind to something—even if we may have previously disagreed with it—a new awareness may appear, bringing with it a new or heightened perspective. True listening allows you to change your mind. It allows you to see something fresh, in a new way. It enables you to say to others or to yourself, "I've never thought of that before." It's the type of listening that creates enjoyment and sharp learning curves. It keeps you in the moment. Listening in this way doesn't cost you anything; there's no downside. You always have the choice to discard later what you have listened to.

Listening, in a sense, is thought recognition. In listening softly we are able to recognize the quality of our thinking, our sensations, our emotions, and life around us. True listening is respectful and loving. True listening enables us to get back on track and return to the moment.

2. SEEING THE WISDOM OF NOT KNOWING

Often, the answer to a problem or dilemma is not immediately obvious, and we simply *don't know* what to do next. As we mentioned earlier, a problem cannot be solved at the same level of thinking in which it was created; we need a shift in our level of understanding. This logic reminds us that if we do not know the answer to a specific problem, recycling the same information over and over usually will not produce a solution. It will, however, keep our minds busy and speeded up. It will create stress. We've all had the experience of being stuck in "thought quicksand," where our mental struggling sucks us deeper into our analytical thinking. This is an example of the misuse of the analytical thought process.

The best way to solve a problem that is not immediately apparent is to tap into our creative thought process, a flow of thoughts that emerges naturally as we empty the mind of our analytical thinking. This deeper intelligence or free-flowing thinking takes us to a higher level of understanding and usually provides us with the answers we need. Being willing to not know, having the humility to admit that our analytical thinking isn't providing us with the answers we need, is the entry point into the free-flowing mode of thinking. Over time, you will begin to trust that this reflective mode of thinking has most of the answers you need.

If we can admit that we are stumped, that we don't know, and if we can learn to become comfortable with this, we will be able to relax in the midst of confusion and spend more of our lives in the moment. We will be living at the speed of life. It may seem ironic, but staying calm in the midst of a storm becomes possible *only* when we trust that *not* knowing is often the best possible means for coming up with an answer. Forcing answers, pretending or convincing ourselves that we know what to do, and using habitual thinking all keep us speeded up, away from the moment and operating too quickly. Often, an insight will occur only when we fully accept that we don't know what's best. "A fool always knows; a wise man never knows."

3. HAVING FAITH IN THE FREE-FLOWING MODE

In order to let go of our churning thoughts, we must know and trust that the free-flowing mode is sometimes more powerful, creative, and effective than our analytical thinking. This is particularly true in situations where we don't have an answer or where we don't know how to deal with a problem. Even for something as mundane as remembering a phone number, directions, or someone's name or address, we must sometimes "let it go" in order for the answer to pop into view. How often have you had the experience of unsuccessfully trying to remember someone's name at a party, then, out of the blue, while driving home it somehow appears in your memory? It's no accident that you remembered something when it was no longer important to you. Our memory and creative thinking process don't perform well under pressure. As we relax and slow down, our free-flowing thinking takes over, all by itself, on its own. We have to do nothing.

Many of us are in the habit of rehearsing our lives. We go over and over what we have to do today, what we did yesterday, or what must be done in the future. We keep our minds busy, speeded up, and preoccupied with a list of shoulds and must-dos so that we are prepared for the unexpected. This habit keeps us in our processing mode of thinking well beyond the point that it is healthy. It prevents us from being open to the moment because our minds are focused on the past or the future. This robs us of spontaneity and responsiveness. Some of us believe that if we aren't constantly processing what to do, we will be inefficient or forgetful. This belief is responsible for much of the speeded-up feeling in our hectic world. We don't have faith that we will remember to stop and get gas when we need it, pay that phone bill on time, or get that memo off to our customer. Yet the truth is, when the mind is relaxed, living at the speed of life, and we trust in the free-flowing mode, we discover an intelligent flow to our thinking that *always* informs us of what we need when we need it. Using the free-flowing mode of thinking will not turn you into an irresponsible, forgetful person. On the contrary, as you slow down you will become less forgetful. You will work and live smarter. Your memory, insights, and creativity will all become more efficient. Instead of rushing around, scrambling, you will remain calm, visibly relaxed.

Having faith in this flow of intelligent thought improves with time. The more we trust in letting go of our analytical thinking, the more room it leaves for a healthy, natural flow of thoughts. Free-Flowing thought is always present to serve us in our daily living—in our household management, career, parenting, and social responsibilities. Faith in the free-flowing mode gives way to knowing that this mode of thinking is the most natural, joyful, and effective way to live our daily lives.

QUIET REFLECTION

The next time you can't remember something—someone's name, a fact, a song, what you were about to do—remember that not having an answer has nothing to do with how intelligent you are. Simply accept that you don't know right now but that the answer will come when you're not so invested—when you care less. See if you can discover the power of *not* trying so hard.

4. PUTTING YOUR PROBLEMS
ON THE BACK BURNER

*The challenge is the thing. I might not get the
answer right away. I might have to walk away,
have a cup of coffee, but when I come back, the
idea comes to me.*

EMIL VOLLMER,
INVENTOR AND PLANT ENGINEER

Occasionally, we listen for an answer to pop up, and nothing
occurs to us immediately, or what does occur does not seem
sufficient. What then? Does this mean that our free-flowing
thinking isn't working? Not at all. In these instances, it's
helpful to put the issue on the back burner.

The back burner of your mind works in much the same
way as the back burner of a stove, slowly brewing a pot of
vegetables and broth into a delicious, succulent feast of soup.
All you had to do was put each of the ingredients in the pot,
stir them up, and then *leave them alone* to cook, only periodi-
cally adding a dash of this or that and stirring the pot. A soup
on the back burner needs to cook slowly; if we cook it too
fast, the flavors don't blend properly or we burn the ingredients. The back burner of a stove requires little attention; we
can cook something else on the front burner at the same
time.

In the same way, we can solve problems with far greater
ease if we feed the back burner. Try setting on your back
burner a pot of problems, possible solutions, facts, and
timetables for when you need an answer. Like the ingredients

of the soup, the thoughts you put on the back burner must be left alone to cook properly while you live in the present moment of daily life.

Putting problems and decisions on the back burner does two things:

1. It allows us to slow down to the moment and attend to what is happening in the now and enjoy our lives.
2. It puts our most creative and intelligent thinking to work on issues that we have no immediate answer for.

For example, Joe was recently talking to a friend who was visibly caught up in her analytical thinking about what to do about a relationship she had become involved in. She was asking herself questions like, "Should I see him anymore? Should we do more together? What will my parents think of him? What do I think of him?" She was feeling anxious, confused, pressured, and frustrated. She was so preoccupied with her dilemma that she had ceased to enjoy his company. It seemed obvious that her analytical thinking was getting in her way; it clearly wasn't serving her well. She felt that she couldn't tell what her heart was trying to tell her.

She needed to give the situation a break and let it sit for a while—put it on the back burner until her feelings became clear. Making the decision to trust her reflective mode of thinking instead of her analytical thought process brought her a sense of relief. Within a short period of time, her feelings became clear and she decided to continue the relationship. Her decision-making process created little, if any, stress for her. Rather than making a hurried, pressured decision, she was able to wait until the answer was clear.

The back burner is *not* an excuse for denial or procrastination. As one colleague of ours said, "Put your problems on the back burner, but don't turn the burner off." In other words, begin with openness and the desire for a solution. Then, simply let go of any thoughts about it. Get out of the way! Your faith in the free-flowing mode will prepare the mind for an insight. The next time the problem comes to mind, it may be a little clearer but not yet complete. If so, put it back again until it is fully cooked or realized. You'll know when the answer is complete. A peaceful feeling, a sense of knowing, will emerge. Allow the answer to become evident.

Another way of looking at this idea is to imagine letting the silt settle in a lake so you can see the lost object on the lake's bottom. There is nothing to do but let our busy thoughts settle so we can see the obvious answer that lies on the bottom of our mind.

IN SLOW MOTION

The next time you have a concern, problem, or challenge that has you stumped, try putting it on the back burner. Tell your back burner the nature of the problem, when you need the solution, and any other specifications you wish. Now, let go! Don't be checking the pot every five minutes. Remember, a watched pot never boils. When your answer comes, remind yourself of the type of thinking that created your answer—free-flowing, back-burner thinking. The more you reinforce the genius of this free-flowing thinking, the more often you will trust yourself to use it.

SPEEDING UP YOUR LIFE: THE PITFALLS

People speed up their lives with their own thinking in three main ways. It may be helpful to briefly list and describe these pitfalls so that you can avoid them as much as possible. They are:

1. Analyzing your problems and your life
2. Judging yourself every time you realize you are out of the moment
3. Living in the past

1. ANALYZING YOUR PROBLEMS AND YOUR LIFE

Obsessing, analyzing, calculating, figuring out, imagining possible outcomes as if they were happening: These are all ways of thinking that will keep you out of the moment and caught up in your thinking. When we use the analytical mode of thinking—incorrectly—we spin our wheels trying to force a solution or a decision. This is the ego's way of trying to predict life instead of being comfortable with the unknown.

There are times, of course, when we *can* come up with an immediate solution through our memory or through recalculating information that we already have available to us. As discussed in chapter 1, the analytical mode is *not* the enemy; it is our servant to be used, as needed, when all the variables are known. The analytical mode is ideally suited for planning, scheduling, calculating, memorizing, and recalling data.

The problem arises when we don't want to admit that all the information is not at our disposal. During these times we need to surrender to the unknown. This act of humble admission that we don't have the answer frees us up to be open to the creative intelligence that lies within.

2. SELF-JUDGING, OR "THERE I GO AGAIN"

At the moment of thought recognition—the moment we realize we are using our thinking against ourselves—we can go one of two ways. We can be graceful (and grateful) that we have realized that we are caught up in our thinking. Or we can chastise ourselves for being so stupid. When we judge ourselves for falling asleep at the wheel of our thinking, we lower our spirits and fall deeper and deeper into our memory and analytical thinking. Judging ourselves only makes matters worse.

When Joe was first learning the principles of Psychology of Mind, he fell into the habit of measuring his progress. He often felt embarrassed that he would still get caught up in his thinking from time to time—as if he should be perfect. Rather than being grateful for his progress, he was frustrated by his lack of perfection.

It is part of the human condition to get caught up in our processing mode. When you catch yourself, say to yourself with compassion and a light heart, "There I go again." You are always just one thought away from healthy thinking. It's less important how often we get off track than how gracefully we get back on track. Self-acceptance is the route to slowing down to the moment.

3. LIVING IN THE PAST

When we spend too much time reliving the past, we are, by definition, not in the moment. Time spent regretting or feeling guilty, embarrassed, or resentful is going to keep you from experiencing the present. Of course there *are* things we regret, feel guilty about, and wish others hadn't done, but spending time thinking about them will increase the chances of repeating the error and the pain associated with past errors.

As professionals, we have witnessed the imprisonment of thousands of innocent people, trapped by living in the past. This is the major cause of mental illness and addiction—the inability to move beyond the past. You can certainly learn from past mistakes and be accountable for your behavior, but try to avoid, as much as possible, keeping your attention in the past. By living more of your life in the free-flowing mode of thinking, you will be able to move on—to live more of your life in the present moment. Each moment, then, can be lived with renewed spirit and insight.

SUMMARY

These pitfalls that keep us from living in the moment—analyzing, self-judging, and living in the past—are habits that we all fall into from time to time. They are so much a part of normal, everyday living that for the most part we are unaware of the tremendous damage that they are doing to us. It is like taking a little poison each day—enough to gradually make us sick and eventually kill us, but not enough to see the reason we are dying. But these pitfalls are psychological killers. They are more subtle than, for instance, an anxiety attack, which would remind us instantly that we are worrying, analyzing, and processing too much. These pitfalls are just destructive enough to keep us away from our mental health and from living in the moment.

By practicing the *healthy* habits of listening, being willing to not know, having faith in the free-flowing mode, and putting problems on the back burner, we will spend more of our time living at the speed of life. Living in the moment helps us slow down from our crazy pace and live our lives guided by wisdom.

CHAPTER 4

Stress and Your Innate Mental Health

Slowing down to the speed of life allows us to see aspects of life that were previously hidden in the frenzy of a busy mind. It allows us to open to the radiant, joyful feelings that reside within. We find that beneath the vicissitudes of our thoughts lies a spaciousness, a peacefulness of being, that is incomprehensible to a mind caught up in analytical thinking or a mind operating too quickly. When our mind isn't racing to the next series of thoughts or holding on tightly to old ones, we gain access to the peaceful feelings of our innate mental health.

There are many times in life, however, when it seems unrealistic, even impossible, to reach a peaceful, loving state of mind. In these times, it can seem that the stress of life is too much to handle and that speeding up is the only answer.

It is the goal of this chapter to share a perspective on stress that will help you slow down to the speed of life, even during stressful times. You will see as you read this chapter that we are talking about stress in a way that is not conventional. As we gain a deeper understanding of healthy psychological functioning, we begin to see where stress really comes from—our own thinking. In this chapter we will see that stress isn't something we catch from the environment or other people; on the contrary, it is something that we quite innocently create by not recognizing the thinking that is creating it. We are not saying that life doesn't produce situations perceived as stressful, such as illness, time deadlines, rush hour traffic, financial problems. What we are saying is that the degree of stress we experience and the actual stress itself originates with our perception of life, which in turn comes from how we are thinking in the moment. By recognizing our thinking and navigating toward a healthy thought process, we can begin to see how, not just to manage stress, but to actually prevent it in our sometimes-hectic lives. This perspective can be achieved by understanding the seven essential steps for reducing the stress in your life.

SEVEN ESSENTIAL STEPS FOR REDUCING STRESS

1. Knowing that inner peace is possible, even in the midst of stressors
2. Having the humility to admit that "getting what you want" isn't the ultimate answer
3. Learning not to deal head-on with or to struggle with problems

4. Understanding that stress originates in your thinking; not getting caught up
5. Learning to not allow passing thoughts to turn into thought attacks
6. Avoiding the temptation to get caught up in the details
7. Lowering your tolerance for stress

1. KNOWING THAT INNER PEACE IS POSSIBLE

Our experiences in life all unfold within the stream of change. Our accomplishments, moments of glory, problems, and difficulties have all come and gone. The same is true with our thoughts. Every thought we have ever had—every neuron that has ever formed—has had a beginning, a middle, and an end. Only one experience in all our lives is always present, although not always experienced: our innate mental health, which rests beneath these changing thoughts and experiences. Although it's seductive (and habitual for most of us) to superimpose fearful, negative, hurried, and insecure thoughts over our mental health, the latter is always potentially present.

All of us experience stress as we go through life, but our experience of stress varies greatly, since it is dependent on our thinking in the moment. Something that feels highly stressful to one person is a delightful adventure to another; only the thought varies. A stressor is anything external to the person that can be perceived as stressful. Our colleague George Pransky tells the humorous story that he once sold T-shirts for two hundred dollars each that he guaranteed "would prevent 100 percent of all stress, other than that originating from the wearer's own thinking, or your money would be happily refunded." He was quite confident he wouldn't be giving any refunds. All experience of stress is the result of thought. Thus it is potentially preventable.

Hope is a powerful force. When you know in your heart that it's possible to feel peace, despite the fact that you aren't experiencing it at present, hope keeps the door open, providing a window of opportunity to slow down to the speed of life and gain access to your healthy psychological functioning.

2. ADMITTING THAT GETTING WHAT YOU WANT ISN'T THE ULTIMATE ANSWER

It's important to understand the distinction between what most people think of as happiness and what is true, lasting contentment. Most people connect happiness with getting what they want. This type of happiness is superficial and temporary. We're happy when we get what we want and miserable when we don't. We spend a lifetime trying desperately to get what we want most and trying equally hard to avoid getting what we don't want. Life becomes a sort of Ping-Pong game we play with ourselves—chasing what we want and darting away from what we fear. Up, down, sideways, and every which way—chasing, always chasing.

At some level, many of us know that our efforts to control that which is inherently uncontrollable cannot yield the happiness we seek. Yet we keep on trying. We fill our minds with thoughts and ideas of what would make us happy. We convince ourselves that we would be happy if only our spouse treated us differently. We would be happy if our bills were paid or if we made more money. We'd certainly be happy if our child received better grades, if the weeds didn't grow so quickly in the backyard, or if we only had more time. The list goes on and on. And each time a desire is fulfilled, we replace it with another, always believing that if the next one would only come true, we'd feel the peace we crave. Each of us has our own list of conditions that must be met before we allow ourselves to feel happy.

There is a direct link between our wish list and our feelings of stress. The more we want something we can't have—or the more we have something we don't want—the greater our feeling of stress. If, for example, you think you need twice the income you currently earn in order to feel secure, you will feel stress each time the discrepancy between what you have and what you want enters your mind. The more desperately you want the extra income, the more stress you feel. Or you might feel stress because you don't feel you have enough time to get everything done on your to-do list. "If only I had more time," you think to yourself, "I would have so much less stress." The more you think about how little time you have, the more convinced you are of the inherent stress in your life.

In these examples and so many others, a typical strategy is to cling to the hope that getting what you want will solve your problems and make you happy. For example, you may hope for a pay raise; when it doesn't materialize, you feel defeated. Or you stay late at the office, trying to catch up on your work, only to realize that it's all but impossible to catch up—there's always more to do than there is time to do it. Or you meet a new person and immediately believe "this is the one," then feel devastated when your new friend turns out to be all too human. You set up a condition in your mind that must be met in order for you to be happy, then use that very condition as ammunition against yourself when it falls short.

Unfortunately, even when your dreams do come true, the peace you feel is short-lived. The same mind-set that created the conditions in the first place will quickly repeat itself. If you manage to make more money, you will quickly find a way to spend it. Soon you'll need even more money. Or you add two hours of additional work to your already long day. Then you discover that despite your extra effort you're still behind schedule. You simply fill up the extra time with even more things to do. Or if the person you meet does turn out to be "the one for you," you'll eventually become concerned about the possibility of that person letting you down. Without awareness of how our thoughts can deceive us, the mind will always find a way to cover up positive feelings with the desire for life to be different than it is.

In order to feel less stress in your life, you must at some level realize that getting what you want isn't usually the ultimate answer. Instead, the only answer is to experience thinking that allows you to feel peaceful whether or not you get what you want.

3. LEARNING NOT TO DEAL HEAD-ON WITH OR TO STRUGGLE WITH PROBLEMS

There are two essential ways to approach the stress in your life. The first way, the one most commonly prescribed, is to deal head-on with your perceived sources of stress. This means that you try to eliminate sources of stress on a case-by-case basis. If, for example, you feel that your marriage isn't as nourishing as it should be, your strategy would be to think about it and try to make it more nourishing. You might visit a marriage counselor, read books on troubled marriages, or attend a weekend workshop that addresses negative relationships. You would analyze the relationship, trying to figure it out. You would think through the problem in an attempt to arrive at a satisfactory solution. Your thoughts might include ideas such as, "If my spouse would listen better, I'd be happier," or "She isn't really interested in what I want." You might come to conclusions such as, "He never really did love me," or "I think we need a divorce." When you try to think through your stress in this manner, you are engaged in process thinking and are speeding up rather than slowing down to the speed of life.

The problem with this head-on method of dealing with stress is that the strategy itself validates and exacerbates the problem. With each book we read and each counselor we speak to, the belief that we are in a stressful situation is reinforced and validated. The more we think about the problem or try to change it, the worse it will seem for the simple reason that we are validating the notion that stress exists outside ourselves. Our thinking keeps us away from the present moment, focused either on the future, where we believe the problem may be solved, or in the past, mentally reviewing the facts that we believe are causing our stress.

If we don't understand where stress actually originates (in our thinking), we will either look for ways to change the so-called source or for ways to cope. In either case, we are fighting an endless battle with little chance of sustained victory. If we can't change our conditions, we can continue to use them as an excuse for our stressful lives. If we do somehow manage to change our circumstances, we only validate the erroneous belief that changing the circumstances leads to being happy. Then, the next time something isn't to our liking, we will once again think that we have to change it. The cycle is endless—and vicious.

The truth is, the moment we define stress as coming from anywhere outside ourselves, we set ourselves up to experience it—and are certainly too late to prevent it. Each time we describe stress as being out there, we validate its existence. We then need to find ways to cope with, manipulate, or, to use today's popular term, "manage" it.

Any effective solution to stress must address the underlying cause, not the details of our problems. The solution must bring us back to our healthy psychological functioning, to the present moment, not take us farther away from it.

4. UNDERSTANDING THAT STRESS ORIGINATES IN YOUR THINKING

Stress is not something that happens to us but rather something that develops within our own thinking. From the inside out, we decide what is and what is not stressful. Events are not stressful per se; they are what we make of them. For example, bungee jumping may be a thrill for one person and the cause of a nervous breakdown for another. Investing in the stock market seems wise to one person and foolish to someone else. Working the suicide hot line seems noble to one counselor and creates great anxiety for another, equally talented, professional.

We saw in chapter 2 that the fact that you are caught up in your thinking is more relevant to the way you feel than are the specifics of what you are caught up about. This understanding is always true, but it is particularly relevant to the study of stress. Most of us are experts at getting caught up in our thinking, particularly when we think something is stressful. You might think, for example, that it's critical that your house be perfectly clean before your guests arrive for the weekend. When it isn't, you begin thinking about how unhappy this makes you. Thoughts like, "My house is never clean," and "What are my guests going to think of me?" begin to fill your mind. If you're not conscious of what's happening, these thoughts will multiply until you're having a full-blown thought attack. If you could step back from the situation and allow your thinking to slow down, you would be able to see that your thoughts were blowing the situation out of proportion. Rather than accepting the moment as it is, you struggle by wishing it were different. Your mind tells you you'd be happy if your house were clean.

"But my house is a mess," you might say, and you might be correct. If you remain calm, however, in the moment, you'll know what to do. You may recall from chapter 2 our example of Richard needing to get his daughter to school in time for his important meeting. Despite the apparent urgency, the best solution was to remain in the moment, not allowing his mind to spin out of control. The same understanding applies here as well. When you approach the situation more calmly, it may look as though not enough is happening. However, you'll notice, upon closer examination, that the perfect level of activity is taking place. You may choose to clean your home, or you may not. When your mind is in the moment and you are moving at the speed of life, rather than reminding yourself how awful the situation is and rushing around frantically deciding what to do next, you'll respond with appropriate and effective action. Rather than feeling over-whelmed and frustrated, you'll simply deal with the situation in the most appropriate manner. You'll do what's before you and get on with your day.

A Story of Present-Moment Living

A few years ago, we had the opportunity to hear an eloquent lecturer speak to the issue of being in a hurry. His story is worth repeating here. During the question-and-answer period, a harried and nervous-looking audience member asked a question about the speaker's schedule: "My gosh, you're busy. You've given lectures in over fifty cities during the last two months. That's almost a city a day! You're crisscrossing the country. How do you do it? Aren't you exhausted? Your schedule would drive me crazy!" There was a sense of panic in the questioner's voice; clearly, this schedule would drive him crazy.

In a sincere voice that calmed the entire audience, the speaker responded very quietly, "I simply do one thing at a time. Rather than looking at my schedule and freaking out that I'll be in New York tomorrow and Cleveland the day after, I simply do what is before me. I wake up, I eat breakfast, I speak to audiences, I get into taxis, which take me to airports, and so on. One thing after another, after another, after another." The speaker was referring, in his own words, to the speed of life, which makes life seem not only manageable but actually peaceful. More than his words, his calm demeanor convinced the audience that life is really nothing more than a series of present moments—one right after another—to be experienced. A schedule becomes an emergency only when it is blown out of proportion—when you analyze it and figure out how many more meetings you have today and how few hours of sleep you're going to get tonight, and so on. The more you think about what you're doing rather than simply doing it, the more urgent your schedule feels.

We've seen that it doesn't matter what you're caught up about. From the perspective of stress, being caught up *is* the problem, although most people believe and would argue that the details are to blame. In truth, the dynamic of stress is the same whether you're dealing with a hectic schedule, a personal bankruptcy, a divorce, or even something trivial such as the height of your neighbor's fence. Whenever you allow your mind to focus on something you don't want or something you believe should be different than it is, you will experience the stressful link between the way you think and the way you feel. Remember, your thinking and feelings are one and the same thing.

Can you imagine what would have happened to the lecturer in the above example had he fretted about his hectic schedule throughout the day and complained about it to his audience and his friends? Instead of being an example of inner peace, he'd be a nervous wreck!

To varying degrees, we all turn ourselves into nervous wrecks many times a day. Whenever we get caught up in our thinking, we are laying the foundation for stress. The more caught up we become, the more stress we feel. Once you understand the dynamic that creates stress instead of trying to eliminate its sources, you'll be on your way to a calmer, more peaceful life. The truth is, stress does not exist, except in your own thinking. Your stressful thoughts are no more real than your nonstressful thoughts; they're just thoughts. Stress is merely your perception of a situation, not the situation itself. When you redefine stress like this—as something you can control—you can maintain a positive feeling even when circumstances don't seem to warrant your optimism.

CONSIDER THE POSSIBILITY

Imagine how different your experience of time would be if you were to live moment-to-moment in the same way that the lecturer did in the above example.

Create in your mind a possible stressful scenario dealing with the many things you have to do—getting ready for work, getting the kids ready, cleaning your home, paying the bills, calling the apartment manager to request a repair, working, attending soccer practice, helping a friend, returning phone calls, and so on.

Now, instead of feeling overwhelmed, imagine how different these events would seem if you forgot about how many things were on the list and instead simply did one thing at a time. Imagine getting yourself ready without thinking about what was next on the list. Then, imagine getting the kids ready without filling your mind about how often you have to do this chore. On and on down the list, one thing at a time without the distraction of your analytical mind.

If you would approach your schedule in this manner, you would discover more joy in these ordinary, daily events than you ever thought possible. You'd also find that a schedule approached in this way is far less overwhelming.

5. LEARNING TO NOT ALLOW PASSING THOUGHTS TO TURN INTO THOUGHT ATTACKS

A single, passing thought will rarely lower our spirits or create stress. The problem is that those harmless individual thoughts can easily multiply into thought attacks if we let them. Our thinking does to stress what water and sunshine do to our gardens: As we dwell on a thought, the object of our attention will grow in our minds. Then, with little awareness on our part, our discontented feelings will suddenly seem justified and real. We can transform a minor annoyance into an enormous source of stress if we think about it enough. This is why so many people get bothered by little things. Blowing things out of proportion can be a deadly habit.

It all starts with a thought. "Kay shouldn't have said that to me." Now that the thought has come to mind, you can do one of two things. You can disregard it as a passing thought, or you can focus on it and make it grow. If you dismiss the thought, it's over and done and you're on to the next thought. At this point, you can calmly decide whether or not Kay's comments are relevant and worth getting into with her, or whether you'd be better off ignoring the matter. By recognizing that it is a thought, you keep yourself operating at the speed of life, one thing at a time. In this more peaceful state of mind, your wisdom will help you decide what action to take, if any.

If you focus on the thought, however, it will begin to grow and you will feel its stressful effects. "Kay shouldn't have said that to me . . . and she has an annoying voice . . . and she's passive-aggressive, too!" You begin to catalog Kay's irritating qualities and remember the times she hasn't been a very good friend. On and on you go. Once you get momentum, a thought attack is hard to control.

Now that you're engaged in a full-blown thought attack, you feel a little angry and stressed out. Instead of living in the present, your thoughts propel you back to all the times Kay has been less than perfect in the past and forward to anticipating her future transgressions.

As simple—and ridiculous—as this seems, this dynamic is played out constantly. We've all heard the classic story of how failing to put the toilet seat up or down can ruin a marriage. In reality, of course, the toilet seat has nothing to do with it. It's our analysis of the situation that causes the distress we feel. The thought, "I wonder why my partner can't remember to do this one simple thing," leads to a series of rapid-fire thoughts like, "He always does things to irritate me," "I can't believe everything I have to put up with," and "I bet he does it on purpose." We work ourselves up, our thinking speeds up, and we've left behind the speed of life.

Such thought patterns occur habitually and automatically, and most of us don't even realize we're entertaining them. Had we noticed how we were thinking before jumping on board the train of thought, the quality of our thinking would have changed. We then could have dismissed the thought as merely a thought—not an emergency—and stayed at the speed of life.

6. AVOIDING THE TEMPTATION
TO GET CAUGHT UP IN THE DETAILS

The details of our thoughts feed our attention and often compound our feeling of stress. If you are in a low mood and have the thought, "I don't care for my neighbor," you can dismiss the thought, table it until you feel better, or feed it by filling in the details. You can think about why you don't like your neighbor, all the things he does to bother you, and how much better off you'd be with other neighbors. Here, as is often true, the details of your thoughts will snowball, increasing your feelings of stress. The more specific you get, the worse you will feel as the pace of your life accelerates. Whatever the situation, the more we use process thinking to address it, the more likely we will be to spiral downward into unhappiness.

The better solution here, of course, is to notice your thinking. When this happens, your head will clear, moving into flow thinking, gently releasing all thoughts pertaining to your neighbor. Let them go. You can always come back to them later, if need be.

Thinking about why we feel stressed—the precise and exact way something bothers us—actually lowers our spirits, increases our experience of stress, and makes our problems seem more formidable. This inner dynamic can, and often does, transform a simple feeling of stress into a major crisis, as you can see in the following example.

Suppose that, outside the grocery store, a disgruntled customer yells at you to move your car. Later in the day, you tell your spouse about the incident. You get right into the details—the sound of the person's voice, the look on her face, how mad you felt, and so forth. As your story gets more specific, you reexperience the feelings you had back in the parking lot, only now they're a lot worse. Here you are, sipping a nice glass of wine with your spouse, yet ruining your evening over an incident that's over and done with. In reality, the problem is now your thought. But it's hard to stop. Because you've gotten yourself all caught up in the details, it now seems imperative to keep thinking about and discussing the incident.

The truth is, the person who yelled at you had nothing to do with the way you feel right now. True, she may have acted inappropriately, but the entire incident lasted just a second or two. Now, hours later, it's only your thinking that is keeping it alive. It is your perception of the details, your speculation about the type of person who would do such a thing and what her hidden motives might be, and all the rest of your negative thinking that have combined to create your unpleasant feeling of stress. In the absence of this thinking, you would simply be, enjoying the moment. Instead of perpetuating the feeling of being a victim, you'd be enjoying the company of your spouse.

Interestingly enough, living at the speed of life doesn't imply that thoughts of the parking lot incident wouldn't cross your mind. In all likelihood, they would. The difference would be that when your attention is in the moment, a train of thought will enter your mind but you won't feel compelled to jump aboard. You'll notice all sorts of stressful thoughts creeping into your consciousness, yet you won't be so quick to give them your undivided attention. Instead, you'll say to yourself, "Ah, there's another one." Instead of reacting to your thinking, you'll maintain a calm, healthy perspective by recognizing thought and remembering that you are the thinker. You'll remember that your thoughts have no power to hurt you unless you take them seriously. They don't have a life of their own. Thoughts are just thoughts. What we make of them, and how we are affected by them, depends on our level of understanding. The higher your level of understanding, the more you realize that thoughts are just thoughts.

CONSIDER THE POSSIBILITY

Can you imagine how different your life would be if, instead of allowing your thoughts to multiply and spiral out of control, you were to simply notice them and let them go? Your feelings of urgency would disappear, and you would begin to calm down. Remember that your thoughts are just thoughts. They cannot harm, frighten, or overwhelm you without your consent.

7. LOWERING YOUR TOLERANCE FOR STRESS

The ultimate solution for stress is to lower our tolerance for it, to recognize it before it becomes a big problem. Once we recognize thought, our thinking slips into a more reflective mode, thus allowing us to see more clearly. This is just the opposite of what many of us have been taught. We've been led to believe that building our tolerance for stress so that we can handle more and more of it is a sign of strength. Unfortunately, the equation is such that our current level of internal stress is always equal to our current level of tolerance. So if you can handle lots of stress, guess what? You'll always feel lots of stress.

Stress is actually a signal that we have gotten into an unhealthy thought process—analytical thinking when it is inappropriate, for example. Seeing stress as a signal can wake us up to the fact that we are thinking, and thus it can shift our mode of thinking. Stress is like the warning light going off in our car, telling us the engine is too hot. Without it, we will damage the engine, our mental health.

It's helpful to think of lowering our stress tolerance in terms of a continuum from one to ten. Assume that level ten represents the highest level of tolerance. A person on this end of the scale will pay no attention to his feelings of stress until it is too late. A heart attack, stroke, or some other major medical emergency will finally awaken him to the fact that his stress level was too high. If this person learned to raise his tolerance further, his skill in avoiding his true feelings could end up literally killing him.

A person at level seven, on the other hand, will catch himself and notice his stress earlier in the process—well before a heart attack, but still too late to prevent a great deal of stress. He might notice that life was overwhelming him only after his wife left him for neglecting his marriage and family, or he might wake up one morning in an alcohol recovery center.

Moving toward the other end of the continuum, people notice their stress signals sooner and sooner. A person at level three might catch herself acting argumentative with her spouse or with someone at work. A person at level two might notice she was beginning to get caught up about something that someone had said to her earlier in the day, and so forth. The ultimate goal is to be able to notice your thinking early, before you allow your stress to spiral out of control. This will create the shift you are looking for. If you find yourself in a very stressed out state of mind, the best strategy is to review the steps outlined in chapter 3, "Getting Back to the Moment."

Remember, the trick in slowing down to the speed of life, very simply, is to notice and recognize our thinking. When we do, we automatically slip into a healthier, calmer mode of thinking—the free-flowing mode.

We have covered seven essential steps to reducing the stress in your life. Let's briefly review them here:

1. Knowing that inner peace is possible. Living at the speed of life is always a possibility. Even when we feel stressed or as if our lives are out of control in any given moment, we can know that it's *possible* to feel better and calmer, even in the midst of chaos. Mental health and inner peace are always close by. Even a moment of thought recognition can guide us back toward tranquillity.

2. Admitting that getting what you want isn't the ultimate answer. We all want things we can't have. There is always the tendency to believe that if we could somehow get what we want, all would be well. If this were true, however, we'd all be visions of peace right now. We have all had many wishes come true, but we continue to struggle. One of the important steps in reducing the stress in your life is to admit that while getting what you want is nice, it *isn't* the ultimate answer. A more powerful, lasting solution is learning to find peace in the midst

of a speeded-up world, even when you can't get what you want.

3. Learning not to deal head-on with or to struggle with problems. As tempting as it can be, struggling with our problems rarely solves them. In fact, the mental struggle itself creates our stressful feelings and gets in the way of gaining access to our wisdom. Dealing head-on with our problems usually speeds up our thinking and validates our erroneous belief that stress is coming from outside ourselves. Learning to find the free-flowing mode is a powerful and productive way to deal with problems.

4. Understanding that stress originates in your thinking. Don't get caught up. As we have said often, being caught up in your thinking is actually more relevant to the stress you feel than is what you happen to be caught up about. By learning to notice when you're getting caught up, you can leave behind your stressful thinking and slow down to the speed of life.

5. Learning to not allow passing thoughts to turn into thought attacks. A single thought can't hurt you or bring stress to your life. Stress is the result of taking our thoughts to heart—taking them too seriously. When you learn to dismiss your speeded-up, stressful thoughts rather than allowing them to turn into full-blown thought attacks, you'll greatly reduce the stress in your life.

6. Avoiding the temptation to get caught up in the details. Remember, the details of your thoughts feed your stressful feelings. Don't overanalyze the specific reasons you are feeling stressed. Instead, use your feelings as a signal to remind you that you've lost sight of your mental

health. If you lose it, remind yourself that all is still okay. Everyone loses it often! Say something simple to yourself like, "Whoops, I lost it again," but don't exacerbate the problem by filling in the details.

7. Lowering your tolerance for stress. Try to notice your stressful feelings earlier in the stress cycle, a process we've called thought recognition. This will create a shift in your thinking and will put you back in the moment. Typically, the longer it takes to recognize your stressful thought, the more difficult it is to get back on track. See if you can notice your stress signals emerging before they ruin your day. If it's too late and you've already lost it, that's okay too! Review the steps in chapter 3, "Getting Back to the Moment."

SUMMARY

All stress begins with a single thought and is thought. What you do next with those initial stressful thoughts determines whether or not the stress will escalate and eventually overwhelm you. If you notice yourself thinking early in the process, before you get caught up—if you experience thought recognition—you are living at the speed of life. Your thinking will shift to free-flowing mode, and you'll be able to get yourself back on track, back in the moment.

The higher your tolerance for stress, the longer it will take to wake up to the fact that your mind is filling with stressful thoughts and moving you away from the speed of life. Instead of keeping your cool, staying calm, and calling on your wisdom, your mind will race a mile a minute, creating well-justified scenarios about how bad everything is, how little time you have to do it all, how difficult other people can be, and so on. People with a very high tolerance for stress have learned not to pay attention to the feelings that signal an impending thought attack. By contrast, if you lower your tolerance for stress—if you can catch your stress-ful thinking before it can carry you away—your thinking will shift and you'll feel better before you know it.

When you focus on the details of your life—what's wrong and who is to blame—your mind moves too quickly to stay at the speed of life. Everything seems like an emergency and is blown out of proportion. But when you keep your bearings by noticing your stressful thinking early in the process, you'll be living at the speed of life. And when you live in a calm state of mind, the same things that used to feel stressful will seem like mere blips on the radar. The thoughts that run through your mind won't seem so compelling and urgent. They will be nothing more than thoughts that have absolutely no power to hurt you or to create stress in your life.

CHAPTER 5

Being Present
in Relationships

Joe recalls the first time he fell in love. It was as though time stopped. Everything seemed brighter, clearer, more alive. He didn't want the feelings to end—joy, laughter, fun, excitement, closeness, a sense of being connected. Every instant seemed precious. When he and his girlfriend were together, he understood the meaning of timelessness. Soon after the relationship began, however, his habitual thoughts of insecurity began to return, creating a barrier to his intimacy. He began to focus on all of their differences and began to question if she was right for him. He wondered whether or not she felt about him the same way he did about her. Needless to say, that sort of thinking soon short-circuited the relationship. Does this sound familiar?

In a way, when we are able to live in the moment, we will feel somewhat like we do when falling in love. Living in the moment shows us our human potential for intimacy. Slowing down to the speed of life in relationships is the essence of ongoing intimacy and love. Slowing down to the moment—whether we have just fallen in love or are enjoying playing with a grandchild—draws out deeper feelings of love, patience, caring, unconditional acceptance, and kindness. When we are able to remain centered in the moment, in our relationships, we experience:

- intimacy
- joy
- spontaneity
- play
- deep listening
- effective communication
- respect
- compassion
- empathy
- kindness
- openness
- gratitude

Slowing down to the moment means that we can experience the presence of another person without the contamination of our analytical mind—without agendas, expectations, preoccupation, resentments, guilt, jealousy, or other negative emotions. When we are operating from a state of effortless thinking, we are able to be touched by that person's presence in a way that seems to increase our understanding of who we are; we feel connected to each other by love. Our mind is not busy; we are not rushing off to be somewhere else or impatiently planning the next activity. Instead, we savor each moment. Our partner feels our compassion, patience, respect, acceptance, and interest.

When Joe had first learned the principles of Psychology of Mind, he had been divorced for a few years and had experienced a series of relationships that fell into a common pattern—falling deeply in love, a honeymoon period, disillusionment, working hard on fixing the relationship, frustration, the end of the relationship. He truly wanted an intimate relationship and read everything he could about the subject. Until he understood the nature of his thinking, however—how his busy thoughts could take him away from his loving feelings—he didn't have a sense of how to allow a relationship to last, deepen, and grow.

About the same time he learned these principles, he met a lovely woman and has been happily married to her ever since. Like every couple, they have had their difficult times, but they have learned to understand how to weather those storms and allow their intimacy to grow. The secret for Joe and his wife has been to learn to recognize their thinking earlier and earlier as they get off track. The two of them have learned the value of being humble enough to admit when they have lost their bearings. As long as they have remained open to gaining a deeper level of understanding, they have been able to grow. Thought recognition has allowed them to see each other with more appreciation, tenderness, compassion, and love. They have learned to see their differences as interesting rather than threatening and have learned to use those differences to help each other grow.

In this chapter we want to explore the connection between thought, living in the present moment, and intimacy.

HEALTHY PSYCHOLOGICAL FUNCTIONING, THE COMMON GROUND

A common ground for everyone is our innate ability to function in a psychologically healthy way. When doing so, we can experience a world of deeper feelings, see another person in fresh, new ways, and look beyond that person's habits to the human potential that lies within. Looking for and seeing mental health in another helps call forth that health out of the other person. When two people fall in love—when they first meet—they are seeing each other in an uncontaminated way. They look beyond their differences, even beyond behavior, to the health that lies within. Often, when we first fall in love, we are in a loving, free-flowing mode of thinking. Being in the free-flowing mode keeps our heads clear of habitual, stereotypical thoughts about the other and allows us to see that person as innocent—as perfect.

By contrast, infatuation is merely a form of attraction based on conditioning. It consists of projecting onto someone else one's own image of the ideal man or woman. When reality sets in, however, infatuated people are quickly disillusioned, as they discover the real person who lives beneath their perceived ideal.

If we could live in the moment and operate in the free-flowing mode most of the time in our relationships, we would rarely lose the feelings of love and connection. Being open to this difficult ideal and resolving to aspire to it are the first steps toward moving in that direction. If you take these steps, the dynamic of your relationships will change, even if you are the only one moving in that direction.

For example, a friend of Joe's recently told him about her father and his recent discovery at age seventy that he had gotten cancer. The doctors told him he had only a short time to live and that he should get his affairs in order. Up to that point, he had been a bitter man. He had lived almost exclusively in his analytical mode, riveted to the past. His mind had been filled with resentments, grudges, and hostility. He had estranged all of his children and most of his friends. The day he received the news from the doctors he came home, and, according to his wife, he stared out the window all afternoon. From that day on, he experienced a complete turnaround, a change of heart. He called his daughter, Joe's friend, and apologized to her for the way he had acted. All of his previous pettiness seemed insignificant now, in light of his imminent death. He woke up to what was truly important in life—his loved ones and his desire to make the most out of each moment he had left. He realized the illusion of the past—how the past was nothing more than thoughts in his mind—and the foolishness of the judgmental thoughts that he had been accustomed to taking far too seriously.

We don't have to wait until we get our own death notice to have this type of awakening or change of heart. And, of course, receiving a death notice doesn't necessarily lead to a realization like this man's. When we learn to live in the free-flowing mode, however, it's almost inevitable that we will have the same or a similar type of experience. Joe's friend said that she had always known that her dad had it in him to be the person he became after receiving his news of cancer. The only thing that had separated him from this feeling was his lack of understanding about the nature of his own thinking.

CONDITIONED THOUGHTS,
THE BASIS OF DIFFERENCES

When we are operating out of our conditioning—our beliefs, ideas, prejudices, opinions, the past—we live in an individual world of separate realities. No two people have the same perceptions, thoughts, or experiences in life, no matter how similar their external realities are. Each of us lives in a separate world of thought, and we see life based on our socialization, past history, and culture. When we are operating out of our conditioned, analytical thinking, we may experience agreement occasionally but rarely true intimacy.

The cause of most arguments is disagreement over what we believe, prefer, or value. The basis of all these is conditioning. By contrast, when we transcend our conditioned thoughts and operate out of free-flowing thinking, we enter the world of common ground—wisdom, common sense, and deeper feelings of love, understanding, and compassion. It is the existence of the free-flowing mode that explains how people of totally different cultures, backgrounds, and belief systems can fall in love, be at peace, and appreciate their differences. This core of intimate feelings is our innate mental health. When we learn to live in the free-flowing mode, we discover the secret to bridging our separate realities. In this next section we will look at the most common cause of getting out of the moment in relationships: the busy mind.

THE BUSY MIND, PREVENTER OF INTIMACY

What prevents our reaching our positive deeper feelings is a speeded-up, busy mind that is unaware that it is off balance.

When the mind is busy and we are not aware that we are thinking, we see life through the distortion of unhealthy thought. When our thinking speeds up, we often feel lonely, alienated from others, and maybe even somewhat misunderstood, mistrustful, or paranoid. Our unhealthy thinking acts like a filter, screening out the light of love in our and others' hearts. The most painful moments and periods in any relationship usually occur when one's head is full of stress—the sign of a busy mind.

LEVELS OF UNDERSTANDING AND RELATIONSHIPS

As we begin to understand how our mind and the different modes of thinking operate in our lives, our level of understanding about relationships begins to increase. At lower levels of understanding, we feel lonely, isolated, and reactive. Others can seem threatening and can appear to be the source of potential hurt. As we feel more secure and are able to recognize our thinking, we begin to see a greater degree of innocence in others' behavior. We start to feel warm and compassionate toward them. These feelings make them, as well as ourselves, feel safer and more secure. Thus others begin to relax in our presence. They lighten up.

As our understanding goes up, all of our relationships change; they actually look different. The way to raise our level of understanding is to simply and calmly notice our thinking. Are we using our thinking against ourselves? Are we having thought attacks? Or are we in a reflective state of mind? Are we using our free-flowing thinking as often as possible?

One of Joe's clients had been contemplating leaving her husband. He had been going through a difficult period in his work and was preoccupied, distant, and unavailable to her. The more distant he became, the more she became demanding and desperate for his attention. And the more desperate she seemed, the more he avoided coming home. They were in a vicious circle of busy mind leading to isolation then anger then withdrawal.

As the therapy process continued, the client began to notice how she was using her thinking against herself—how her speeded-up thinking was interfering with her loving feelings. As this happened, she began to feel less depressed and desperate. This enabled her to pressure her husband less often. She realized that by using her free-flowing mode of thinking instead of creating battles in her mind using her analytical thinking, she could experience her mental health even as her husband was going through a difficult time. She realized that her happiness was not dependent on how her husband was acting—or even on how happy he was. By simply noticing her thinking more and more often, her level of understanding changed. Instead of feeling needy, she began to feel compassion for him.

One night her husband came home late after a particularly difficult business trip. When he walked in the door, she realized that he was exhausted and stressed. In fact, he looked beaten and frustrated. Her heart went out to him, and she opened her arms to embrace him. For the first time in eighteen years of marriage, he cried and allowed himself to be comforted. He ended up sharing and speaking intimately with her for three hours.

Since then, they have reestablished their commitment to

one another and are closer than ever. They have learned to slow down to the speed of life, to take time for each other, to listen, and to love. Upon reflecting on her story, Joe's client began to see how her feelings of urgency, neediness, and anger had literally kept him away.

The following chart demonstrates how our vision of a relationship changes as our level of understanding increases.

LEVELS OF RELATIONSHIPS

Impersonal Love/Bliss
Unconditional Love/Joy
Compassion/Healing
Warmth/Kindness

Bother/Irritation
Anger/Conflict
Hatred/Violence
Indifference/Isolation

The terms used in this chart are not meant to be absolute stages of relationships; rather, they are arbitrary terms to describe the general evolution of relationships as our level of understanding rises. As we have said earlier, why, when, and how a level of understanding rises is a mystery. However, we do observe that a sincere desire to change, coupled with the understanding of the concepts explained in this book, seems to increase the occurrence of these vertical jumps in our understanding. Humility, patience, and an open mind are also great fertilizers for realization.

At the lowest level of understanding, relationships are painful and abusive, and there is an absence of love. People are too insecure to trust others or even believe they are lovable. Still very negative is the level of relationship that includes a connection, but with feelings that are full of hatred and even violence. The difference is that there is some level of relationship, albeit negative. As the level of insecurity lessens, the level of violence is absent, but unresolved conflict is common—there are resentments and distance with periods of some closeness. At the highest level of understanding below the line of mental well-being, a relationship is marked by feelings of caring but mixed with many feelings of bother, irritation, judgment, disappointment, and fear of rejection.

As people in relationships move above the line, their fear of intimacy and doubts are replaced with a feeling of security. This feeling allows the natural feelings of warmth and kindness without expectation of reciprocity to prevail. At higher levels the healing feelings of compassion, understanding, and unconditional acceptance are normal. Forgiveness is natural at this level. As we go up even higher in our level of understanding, our relationships are filled with joy, humor, tenderness, and unconditional love. At the highest levels, we feel an impersonal feeling of love toward all people, without judgments, expectations, or set patterns of interaction. Our relationships are spontaneous, warm, and inspiring.

MOODS IN RELATIONSHIPS

Understanding moods is as important to people in relationships as understanding weather is to an airplane pilot. Moods affect all aspects of our intimate relationships: how we communicate, resolve conflict, make decisions, experience intimacy. These fluctuations in the quality of our moment-to-moment thinking are, of course, a natural and unavoidable part of life. Different moods present our mates in different lights: One minute he (or she) is the most precious person in the world; the next minute we can't imagine why we got together in the first place.

As we gain a deeper understanding of our moods and the moods of people around us, we are protected—to a large degree—from their adverse affects by an emotional umbrella that shelters us, as it were, from the rain. Understanding moods protects us from taking our significant other's interactions seriously when she or he is in a low mood. It also helps us know when to keep our mouths shut and when to warn others that our internal weather forecaster sees a storm brewing.

There are several guidelines to dealing with our and others' moods:

1. When you are in a low mood, take your perceptions of other people with a grain of salt. In low moods we tend to be serious, judgmental, critical, bothered, impatient, and irritated. We see others as less attractive and as uncooperative, and we attribute ulterior motives to their actions. If we recognize that our thinking is responsible for these perceptions, we can see the need to make an adjustment in our attitude. If we wait out the storm and let our mood pass, we always see that it was our process thinking that was distorting our perception. It is almost comical, in hindsight, when we look at the other end of a low mood.

Seeing our perception in a low mood as questionable is a lot like looking into the passenger-side mirror of an automobile—the one that says "objects may be closer than they appear." We make a quick mental/perceptual adjustment to take into account the distortion in our thinking. When we recognize that we are in a low mood, it may be helpful to warn other people in close proximity that a low mood has arrived and that they should not take it personally. A friend of ours even had a T-shirt made for her husband; it said, "Leave me alone, I'm having an emotional fit!" You may not need to go that far, but you may find that acknowledging a low mood helps to keep the air clear with significant others.

2. Don't take other people's low moods personally. Instead of being defensive, judgmental, or frightened of their moods, try to have some compassion. Being patient with another's moods isn't something you can "think" your way into. You have to see that your mate is just off; no big deal—it happens to the best of us. Wait a few minutes or hours, and you'll be in a low mood too! Then perhaps you'll appreciate someone else's patience and understanding. Try to see another's negativity as impersonal, even when it is directed at you personally. We call this notion "low mood immunity." Understanding protects us from "catching" someone else's low mood. In truth, other people's low moods have absolutely nothing to do with us; they are a product of their thinking.

The other day Joe called his son on the phone just to say hello. His son was cold, unresponsive, and seemed bothered that he had been interrupted. Joe's first reaction was to feel annoyed with his rudeness. Joe sensed his mood was low and decided to ask him how his day was. His son proceeded to tell him how exhausted he was and how he couldn't wait to go to bed. Joe's feeling changed from annoyance to compassion. His son sensed his genuine love and thus began to share several things about his week; he opened up his heart. Joe's compassion opened the door to an intimate moment.

3. Don't try to make decisions or communicate about difficult or important subjects when either you or your partner is in a low mood. We often feel a sense of urgency and seriousness when we're in a low mood, but we should be wary of making any decisions, talking about important matters, and having any kind of important discussion when we're in a negative frame of mind. Know that this feeling of urgency is an emotional signal to alert us that we are out of the moment and have stepped onto Caught Up Avenue. Wait until the emotional weather clears and you are both walking on Serenity Lane instead.

COMMUNICATION: HEART-TO-HEART OR HEAD-TO-HEAD?

In therapy, couples often report that the problem in their relationships would be solved if they could only "communicate better." There is some truth to this but also some misconceptions about communication. Good communication alone will not necessarily improve a relationship. Some communication leads to greater misunderstanding; some can actually end a relationship, causing pain that can take years to get over. At other times communication becomes the turning point of a relationship and leaves both people feeling warm and close. What's the difference?

Communication that comes from the heart has the ability to transform. Heart-to-heart communication helps us get past our separate realities to the common ground of mental health. It helps our thinking evolve and helps us see issues in a different perspective. When two people are communicating heart-to-heart, they always feel more respect and caring afterward than before they spoke.

On the other hand, head-to-head communication— debating, arguing, lecturing, engaging in emotional venting, confronting—doesn't usually have a positive, lasting impact on another person. People usually leave a head-to-head discussion more convinced that they are right and that the other person is uninformed, stupid, or crazy. Head-to-head discussions are generally unproductive and, at their worst, can end disastrously with emotional upset and residuals of guilt and resentment. In a head-to-head discussion, people are talking from their preexisting belief systems and habits rather that from wisdom and insight. This leads to impasse. Discussions are circular and predictable. Couples can usually accurately finish each other's sentences in a head-to-head discussion because they have heard everything a hundred times before. Obviously, head-to-head discussions are not good, effective communication for relationships.

If heart-to-heart communication is more effective at resolving troublesome emotional issues in a relationship, how can we have them? Most of us have experienced heart-to-heart communication at some time in our lives—a special chat with a college roommate, an intimate talk during a time of crisis, a moment of truth between a parent and child. These special talks are rare in most people's lives. By slowing down to the speed of life, however, you can learn to make them an integral part of your life. A heart-to-heart talk has several elements or qualities:

- Each party is respectful and works to establish rapport.
- Both parties are touched deeply.

- Each party listens without interruption and seems to draw the other person out.
- The words come from the heart (free-flowing thinking) in a spontaneous, unrehearsed, or nonhabitual manner.
- Both people feel a greater level of intimacy, and the exchange is usually very memorable.

Heart-to-heart communication may seem mysterious and out of our control, but the more we understand about how to be in the moment and operate from healthy psychological functioning, the more heart-to-heart talks seem to happen. The following suggestions will help you prepare for communication that's effective:

1. Find your own bearings first; get into the free-flowing mode.
2. Let go of any expectations of a particular outcome.
3. Get permission from the other person.
4. Speak from the heart.
5. Listen with nothing on your mind.
6. Stay on track; keep the tone respectful, warm, and compassionate.

Let's discuss each suggestion in some detail.

1. Find Your Bearings

If you are feeling urgent, serious, and impatient, you are in your head—your processing mode. You may need to have a heart-to-heart talk, but it won't happen until you're in your own heart. Wait until your mood rises; the issue will likely still be there when your mood comes up, and you'll be in a better position to change things if you have your bearings. Unfortunately, most people have their most important communications when they have lost their bearings. For a heart-to-heart talk to occur, you must be in the free-flowing mode when speaking and when listening.

2. Let Go of Any Expectations of Outcome

If you have an expectation of a particular outcome, the other person will sense this. The expectation will lead to controlling, manipulating, and pressuring the other person, which in turn will encourage your partner to get into his or her head and become defensive. Expectations lead to disappointment if things don't go exactly as we expect, which, of course, they never do. Disappointment will lower your spirits and put a damper on the communication.

Instead of having any particular idea of outcome, have faith that if you get the proper feeling (rapport) between you and you both talk from the heart, you will see a solution that neither of you had previously considered but that meets the needs of both of you. Having faith in the free-flowing mode in communications will lead you in the direction of a heart-to-heart talk.

3. Get Permission

You may feel that you have your bearings, that you are in the free-flowing mode. You may also feel that you are free of any expectations and are ready for a heart-to-heart. But remember, it takes two to tango. Before you launch into your heart-to-heart, you must get permission from the other person, or you may end up with a heart-to-head. Asking permission does several valuable things:

- It shows respect.
- It alerts the other person to the importance of the communication and thus helps that person get his or her bearings.
- It lets you know if the timing, mood, or level of rapport are off and if you need to be patient until the timing is right.

If you don't take the important step of getting permission, trying to communicate effectively will be like trying to walk through a doorway without opening the door. You may need to reassure the other person of your positive intentions and of your care, or you may need to explain why it is important to you. If you can't get permission, it's best to wait. You may simply need to accept that the other person isn't yet ready.

4. Speak from the Heart

Speaking from the heart means communicating from the free-flowing mode. Speaking from the heart means not thinking about or rehearsing what you are going to say, not thinking about how the other person will react, and not anticipating a response. It's being yourself and letting the words come through you. Speaking from the heart is speaking from inspiration, off the cuff, extemporaneously, or spontaneously. In the free-flowing mode of thinking, the words come out right, taking into account such matters as the frame of reference of the other person, the level of rapport, the tone, and the extent of the permission granted. Speaking from the heart brings our wisdom into the picture.

When people listen from the heart, they demonstrate their high level of interest and respect. The better the listening, the more it seems to draw out the other person; the more someone talks from the heart, the more the other seems to listen.

5. Listen with Nothing on Your Mind

To listen with nothing on your mind is to listen from the heart—listening from the free-flowing mode. The mind in free-flowing mode is more like a radio receiver than it is a computer. It's receiving all the incoming data without analyzing, processing, or rejecting it. In free-flowing mode you don't interpret from a belief system, you don't judge, and you don't anticipate what will be said next. You simply listen nonjudgmentally, trying to take in what the other person is saying. When you listen from the heart, the head is clear. You allow yourself to be affected by the essence of what the other person is saying—not by the words but by the feelings behind the words. Listening from the heart means being truly interested in what the other person is saying. You are not distracted with other thoughts or memories that have been triggered by the conversation. You have no agenda, no expectations, no outcome in mind. Your job when listening from the heart is to be affected by the other person.

6. Stay on Track

While in the midst of a heart-to-heart talk, it's important to keep the emotional tone on track with a tone that is respectful, warm, and compassionate. Irritation, defensiveness, and distraction take you off track. It's also possible to get off track by losing permission as you move into deeper and/or more significant areas of discussion. Keep checking in. You or the other person may have lost your bearings. If any of these things occur, stop until you are both back on track emotionally. Regain your bearings, regain permission, and listen from the heart.

Heart-to-heart communication is a process, not a formula. Every heart-to-heart talk will be entirely different. It takes a leap of faith each time you have a heart-to-heart—a degree of trust in both parties. As our trust in the free-flowing mode increases, we will naturally fall into heart-to-heart discussions when they are needed or appropriate. These guidelines are like training wheels for healthy and effective communication—for present-moment, intimate relationships.

GETTING A FRESH START IN RELATIONSHIPS

To get a fresh start in a relationship, we need to see our partner and ourselves in a new light. This new light is a new way of thinking about life—a whole new perception. Some have called this shift a change of heart or falling in love again. Whatever it is called, it seems to change the way we feel about the past and increases the optimism we feel about the future. Although we don't seem to have any control over when and how this change of heart occurs, a few guidelines can increase the chances of its occurring, just as preparing the soil in a garden can ensure a healthier crop. These four guidelines are meant to help prepare the soil of your relationship for a new beginning.

1. Find hope.
2. Recognize your thinking.
3. See past your habits to the innocence in your partner and in yourself.
4. Forgive and forget.

Let's examine each guideline in some detail.

1. Find Hope

When we are discouraged in our relationships, we tend to slip into unhealthy analytical thinking; we see only aspects of the other person that validate our preconceptions and reinforce why the relationship is hopeless. To reverse this process takes a leap of faith. We must assume that no one has intentionally set out to destroy the relationship—in fact, everyone is doing the best she or he can given the present level of understanding. If we remember that each of us is innately healthy, we can consider the possibility that everyone has the potential to change. "Hope springs eternal" when we can clear our minds of unhealthy analytical thinking and let the hope float to the surface. Our mental health is buoyant; when it rises it brings with it the hope we need to carry on. When our level of understanding rises, we naturally experience the feeling of hope because we see unlimited possibilities unbound by the past.

Hope gives us the psychic strength to carry on in situations that seem hopeless. One of us recently saw a client who came to therapy after being married for less than a year. She was very disappointed in their sex life, and she was becoming resentful and distant. Her husband was scared and had begun to isolate himself from her. She began to fear that her second marriage would end as had the first, with a great deal of abuse, anger, and despair. After that disastrous ending, she had avoided a male-female relationship for many years but finally had fallen in love and thought this one would be different. Now it seemed that she was wrong. "All men are jerks!" she shouted the first session.

As she began to realize that her feelings were coming from her thinking, her mood began to lift and she began to sense her husband's fear. She backed off, and he began to be interested in her again sexually. She didn't mention the sexual problem again until a few sessions later, when she remarked how great sex was now and how she hadn't had to do anything for it to happen other than to change herself. She began to feel hope that no matter what difficulties she and her husband would have in the future, they would be able to handle them, knowing that change begins with a change in thinking. As her spirits have soared, the issues that seemed insurmountable between her and her husband are falling away one by one and exposing the deep love that exists between them.

Every relationship has the potential for transformation. A change in the level of understanding of even one person can put hope into the equation of love and shift the balance from despair to optimism.

2. Recognize Your Thinking

It takes a great deal of humility to recognize that each of us develops thinking habits, some of them unhealthy, that are operating outside of our awareness, on autopilot. Recognizing that we have innocently accumulated some habits that block the love in us frees us from their power. Recognizing our habits is similar to exposing mold to the sunlight—it vanishes.

Take Jack and Julie, for example. Jack had the habit of not listening to Julie when an issue came up. He assumed that she was going to criticize him (which she had been doing for years) and would interrupt her to defend himself. She, in turn, would become more harsh because she was frustrated by his inability to listen. She felt ignored. He felt attacked and became defensive. She turned up the volume and intensity so he would finally listen to her. Both habits fed into each other and spiraled them downward into heated and unproductive arguments. Years of this led to hopelessness and despair. Once they each began to recognize their habits of thought through learning to slow down and listen, they were shocked to discover how each had contributed to the marriage problem and how totally in the dark they were about their own thinking habits. By slowing down, they began to recognize their habits of thought and to navigate together toward their healthy feelings of love for each other.

3. See the Innocence in Yourself and Others

When we look at our relationship and evaluate what has gone wrong, when we wonder why we don't feel the way we once did, we rummage through our memory banks looking for data to explain the discrepancy. This inevitably leads to a perception that someone is right and someone is wrong and to judgments about who made mistakes and what intentions people had all along. These perceptions in turn lead to feelings of blame, resentment, anger, hurt, guilt, shame, self-doubt. The problem with overevaluating your relationship is twofold:

- It is usually self-serving and biased and therefore inaccurate.
- It is based on your thoughts about the situation, which will be self-validating and self-fulfilling.

Another approach is to find the innocence in each other. You do this by assuming two things:

- Both of you are doing the absolute best you can given your present and past level of understanding of life.
- If either of you had your way, you would have total fulfillment, intimacy, and happiness. Ignorance of how to do this is the only impediment.

If we accept these two assumptions (and who doesn't?), we will begin to see the innocence in ourselves and our partner. In some ways it's more important to see our own innocence first, because it makes us less defensive and more relaxed and thus more able to see the innocence in others. Seeing the innocence in another doesn't mean that you and that person aren't responsible for past events or actions. It simply means that each of us is always acting on the choices we are able to see at the moment, given how we see life. In the same way that a starving person thinks only about food or a frightened person sees signs of danger, our reality is tainted by our present state of mind.

Joe remembers as a child seeing a dog hit by a car in front of his house. He wanted to go up to the dog to help it, but as he got closer the dog growled and tried to bite him. He couldn't believe the dog didn't sense his positive intentions and was instead seeing him as potentially harmful. Later, Joe's dad explained to him that injured animals often react that way. Knowing this helped Joe not take the dog's action personally and not dislike the dog.

When human beings are insecure, we act like that dog. We misinterpret help from our mate as manipulation or insincerity, and we react in a less than appreciative manner. When we can recognize that we are feeling negative and can step back, we will regain our perspective. We will be able to take the other person's negative behavior less personally and to accept their positive behavior at face value.

Another tendency we have when feeling defensive and insecure in our relationships is to see a situation in terms of right and wrong, black and white. But doing this locks us into our belief system and predisposes us to becoming analytical. This, in turn, keeps us out of the free-flowing mode, caught up in our beliefs and assumptions. We then tend to judge other viewpoints as stupid, crazy, cruel, morally wrong, and so on. These judgments are contrary to seeing the innocence in another person.

4. Forgive and Forget

Hurts and transgressions accompany all relationships. But the most damaging thing that can happen in any relationship is letting resentments build up. To forgive is to forget. Forgiveness is recognizing the innocence in our or another person's action in the past. When we forgive we are seeing that the person acted at a level of understanding where his or her behavior made sense at the time or seemed like the only alternative.

We forgive another person primarily for ourselves. If we don't let go of a resentment, anger, or hateful feeling, we are stuck with the effects of that feeling, and we begin to contaminate our own life. Our own heart becomes full of negativity, which takes up space and leaves less room for love. We have no room to live in the moment when our minds are dwelling on a past resentment. Our therapy practices bring us countless people who haven't forgiven a parent or other relative or former mate, and the feelings inevitably spill over into their current relationships directly or indirectly. You can't hang onto a resentment and not have it affect your life adversely in some way.

People hang on to past resentments and hurts for three main reasons:

1. To avoid repeating the past. People mistakenly believe that refusing to forgive another will help them avoid repeating the past. They often say that if they forgive others they will get hurt again. When we do not forgive, we go through life trying not to repeat the past.

2. To avoid condoning the behavior. Some people believe that if they forgive the other person or themselves, they are in some way condoning what was done. They fail to see that they can still hold others and themselves accountable for past behaviors—without the negative feelings. The truth is, if you forgive others and *then* share with them your feelings, they will be more likely to listen to you nondefensively. If you confront others with judgment, they will most likely get defensive, not

be able to hear you, and even find something to blame you for. This keeps the cycle going: blame-resentment-defensiveness-transgression.

3. Because they believe that anger motivates them to change the relationship. People hold onto grudges because they think the anger gives them energy to change things in the future. They believe that people who are happy—living in the moment—won't do any-thing about all the problems in the world or in the rela-tionship. This is far from true. When we try to change a relationship out of anger or hate, it destroys the feelings of rapport and sets people up in opposition to each other. It also keeps us from the creative thought process that can lead to change and transformation in a relation-ship.

Forgiveness decontaminates the mind so we can live in the moment and slow down to the speed of life. When we see that resentments are just thoughts held in our memory, and when we see that we have the capacity let go of them, we are on our way to forgiveness. There are three steps to forgive-ness:

1. See the value of forgiveness in your life. If you want a fresh start in a relationship, you must clear your mind of any past experiences that are contaminating the present moment. In order to gain access to the free-flowing mode, you must let up on the button of analytical think-ing. In order to feel happy and creative and to live in the moment fully, letting go of the past is imperative. Many people, however, have the opposite view, believing that

grudges make them strong so they won't easily be made a fool of again. Ask yourself, would you rather justify your resentment or be happy? Would you rather be self-righteously angry or have a loving relationship? On our deathbeds most of us would gladly let go of past hurts. Why wait?

2. Be willing to forgive. Willingness is being open to a change of heart. It gets you to the bus stop of forgiveness. You can't control when the bus will come, but you'll be there when it arrives. Willingness takes you in the direction of forgiveness. If you sincerely want to forgive, whenever the memory of the hurt comes to mind you will say to yourself, "Here is that memory again. I sure look forward to the day when I can see it differently." This acknowledges it as a memory and not as an in-the-moment reality. For years Joe hoped that he would forgive his father for certain omissions, but he attached certain strings to the forgiveness. He wanted his father to admit that he had done Joe wrong. As long as you hold conditions for forgiveness, it puts healing under the control of others. Remember who made up the conditions— you did! Be willing to forgive to get a fresh start.

3. See forgiveness as a process, and know that it will get easier and easier each time the memory comes to mind. If you see the value of forgiveness and are willing to forgive, each time the memory comes to mind while you are in a state of healthy psychological functioning, the experience will be a little less painful. Imagine that reexperiencing a memory is like rinsing dirty laundry in clean water. With each rinse the laundry leaves a little more dirt behind and is a tiny bit cleaner. If the water is

dirty—if you are in unhealthy analytical thinking—the laundry won't get clean no matter how many times you wash it. If, on the other hand, you see the hurt as a memory that is on its way out, your water will be clean and your memory will be healed and understood from a higher, more impersonal perspective.

Joe had a client who had been sexually abused by her brother. All her life she had hated him. Later he committed suicide after a life of drug addiction. As she learned to see the value of forgiveness and became willing to forgive him, her painful memories and nightmares eventually ended. She entered a healthy, lasting relationship, which changed her lifetime pattern of short-lived relationships.

Forgiveness is a necessary, ongoing part of relationships, since we are all fragile and only human. We will always be needing to clean our own windshield, to see others with a fresh perspective. If you practice these steps in your relationships, you too will be able to have a new beginning in any relationship.

SUMMARY

Being truly present in relationships—slowing down to the moment—is the key to intimacy, satisfaction, and effective, loving communication. When we are engaged in an unhealthy use of our process thinking, we tend to view other people from our individual separate reality. Rediscovering our healthy psychological functioning creates the common ground where we can connect with another.

As our level of understanding rises, so too does the quality of our relationships. Understanding moods, separate realities, and thought recognition leads to heart-to-heart, effective communication. A heart-to-heart talk involves being in the free-flowing mode of thinking, letting go of expectations, getting permission, talking from the heart, listening with nothing on our mind, and knowing how to stay on track.

Some of us may have lost hope that a significant relationship can come back to life. We discussed four guidelines to help turn your relationships around: find hope, recognize your thinking habits, see innocence in yourself and your partner, and forgive and forget. Last, we talked about the stages of forgiveness.

In the next chapter we'll examine a specific application of slowing down in relationships that affects most of us deeply—parenting.

CHAPTER 6

Peaceful Parenting

Those of us who have children know how quickly they grow up. One minute they're keeping us up at night, and in what seems like the next minute they would rather be out at night. One minute all they want to do is spend time with us, and the next we are the last people they want to be with.

Yet despite knowing how short is the time we have with them, most of us seem to speed through our parenting years, almost wishing them away. We tell ourselves, "I'll be happier when the infant state in over"; "I'll be relieved when we're out of the terrible twos"; "It will be so much better when the teen years are over." But, ironically, as our children grow up, we convince ourselves of the opposite by rewriting our personal history. "It was so much nicer when the kids were little"; "I miss the baby stage"; "I long for the days when my kids took me seriously." In short, we miss most of the present moments of our parenting experience by focusing our attention on thoughts of the future or memories of the past. Our minds are spinning a mile a minute, trying to get everything accomplished. We go back and forth between believing that "someday" will be better than today, and convincing ourselves that "yesterday" was better than it really was. Rather than immersing ourselves in the present moments of our experience, we keep ourselves one step removed from life with our own thoughts, rarely living at the speed of life.

In addition to working with hundreds of clients who have children at every imaginable age, the two of us have children at opposite ends of the child-raising spectrum. Joe has a twenty-one-year-old son who is out of the house and on his own. Richard has two daughters, ages eight and five. We've found it interesting to discover that the principles of slowing down to the speed of life apply to raising children of any age. Slowing down allows you to step back, gain access to your wisdom, and respond appropriately to the moment at hand. It also allows you to appreciate the different types of joy that children of different ages have to offer. Slowing down to the speed of life allows you to enjoy watching your child grow up and move away from the home as much (albeit differently) as it allows you to appreciate taking your six-year-old daughter to her first discovery museum or watching your one-year-old son take his first steps.

Slowing down to the speed of life so powerfully enhances the raising of children that we have worked with parents who find raising supposedly impossible teenagers to be every bit as wonderful and rewarding as raising a tranquil eight-year-old. By learning to live in and appreciate this moment, regardless of how it may be unfolding, instead of reliving memories of the past or anticipating moments yet to be, you too can transform your experience of parenting into a peaceful one.

As you live more of your life in your healthy psychological state and learn to think in healthier ways, you too will find that the varied challenges that parenting brings to your life don't have to overwhelm you. As you begin to slow down to the speed of life, you'll be able to roll with the punches while at the same time acting appropriately to the moment at hand. The issues of parenting will appear different, easier.

THE EFFECTS OF SPEEDED-UP PARENTING

Before we get into the how-to of slowing down as a parent, let's consider why it is important to slow down. Several serious consequences follow from busy-minded, speeded-up parenting. Here are some of them:

1. You become habitually reactive instead of responsive.
2. You take negative behavior personally rather than seeing the innocence.
3. Little events become front-page news.
4. You miss the good times.
5. You lose sight of your compassion.
6. You expect too much from your children.

Let's take a closer look at each of these consequences of speeded-up parenting.

1. YOU BECOME HABITUALLY
REACTIVE INSTEAD OF RESPONSIVE

A busy, speeded-up mind is also a nervous, agitated, easily rattled mind. When your mind is operating at too quick a pace or when you are taking your own thoughts too seriously, the slightest deviation from your plans or the smallest obstacle can seem like a major catastrophe. Rather than responding appropriately, in the moment, you quickly blow things out of proportion, feeling agitated and annoyed. As your mind moves away from the present moment, you move further away from effectiveness and toward greater reactivity. The faster your thoughts carry you away, the quicker your agitated feelings translate into angry or frustrated behavior, which can further fuel whatever issue engages you and your child. This dynamic is true regardless of whether your child is a restless two-year-old or an apathetic teenager.

Consider this: If a visiting friend spilled a glass of juice on the kitchen table, you'd probably respond by saying, "Don't worry about it. We'll just clean it up. Would you like another glass?" But if your child did the exact same thing, you may react quite differently: "How can you keep spilling juice all over the floor? That's the third time you've done that this week!" As your mind moves away from the moment and begins to review how often this incident has taken place or rehearse how many times it's likely to happen again, negative feelings are the predictable result. In short, a reactive mind is like a beehive filled with buzzing bees and no room to spare. At any moment, your mind is likely to burst—and when it does, chaos results.

A responsive mind, operating at the speed of life, however, is very different. A responsive mind takes things as they come. A spilled glass of juice is just that: a spilled glass of juice. Nothing more, nothing less. No thought is added. And the same is true with more significant issues as well. If your child gets into trouble and your mind is calm, you're going to be in a better position to help than if you're rushing around with a head full of concerns, mentally reviewing past errors or anticipating future problems.

To be an effective parent, you need to maintain your bearings and be able to respond to each challenge as it arises without the distraction of a reactive mind. Thought recognition is the key to remaining in a responsive state of mind and living at the speed of life. Thought recognition creates a shift in your thinking, enabling you to keep your perspective.

2. YOU TAKE NEGATIVE BEHAVIOR PERSONALLY

Another effect of a speeded-up mind is a tendency to take behavior, especially negative behavior, very personally. When your mind is spinning a mile a minute, you will have myopic vision, focusing only on how behavior is affecting you. You'll have a tendency to impute motives to your child's behavior. When your child is acting out, for example, you'll tend to believe that the negative behavior is either being done on purpose as a way to get back at you, or you'll believe that the behavior is a reflection of your poor parenting skills. Frenetic, busy-minded thinking usually leads to taking your own thoughts too seriously. Because your thoughts are firing so quickly, you don't have enough time for needed reflection. Therefore, you react to your own thoughts, turning what could be passing thoughts into full-blown thought attacks. A thought like "Gee, I wish the kids wouldn't fight so much" quickly becomes "My kids are always fighting. What's wrong with them? What have I done wrong?" One thought leads to another and then another, until the stress of parenting seems too much to handle. You lose perspective.

It's difficult to see the innocence of another when your mind is busy analyzing and calculating motives and agendas. A busy mind can convince you that the actions of your children are due to some innate fault in them or in you. If your teenager wants privacy and your mind is moving too fast, it may be difficult to keep your perspective as you will have a tendency to read into the situation. You may react with thoughts like, "Why does he hate me?" or "What have I done wrong?"

A mind operating at the speed of life, however, can see things as they really are. Slowing down gives you needed perspective during times of transition and stress. When you operate at the speed of life and your child desires privacy, you'll probably remember that almost all teenagers go through phases of wanting space from their parents. You probably did too at that age. Rather than take it personally, you'll be able to see the bigger picture. If you are operating at the speed of life and you have the thought, "I wish the kids wouldn't fight so much," you'll likely be able to have the thought without a great deal of mental ambush. You'll remember the potential your thinking has to blow this thought out of proportion. You'll remember that you are the thinker and, as such, you have the power to control your thoughts. If you do lose it, thought recognition will guide your thinking back to the speed of life.

3. LITTLE EVENTS BECOME FRONT-PAGE NEWS

When your thinking is speeded up, little things can easily become front-page news. For example, your child may say something you don't approve of—"I hate school." Rather than take it in stride, you'll embellish the statement into something even bigger. "What do you mean, you hate school? Learning is important. You need school to make it in life. What's the matter with you?" Your child's little statement, probably made in a low mood, becomes headline material in your mind. Rather than hearing "I hate school" and leaving it at that, you turn it into important news, "Child Hates School." For details, turn to page six!

When your mind is moving too quickly, events as well as your own thoughts about those events become much larger than they really are. This makes you lose perspective, which, in turn, makes maintaining rapport with your child all but impossible.

Again, the solution is to slow down your thinking and remember that you are the thinker who is blowing this event out of proportion. As your mind slows down to the speed of life and as you have thought recognition, your thinking shifts into the free-flowing mode and you are able to remember the role that your own thinking is playing in the scenario. When your mind is thinking too quickly, life appears to be happening to you, but when you slow down, you can see your part in the process.

4. YOU MISS THE GOOD TIMES

As therapists, we've seen hundreds of parents who have missed some of the most precious moments of raising their children. A year or so ago Richard was on a beach in Hawaii with his wife and two children. Two couples were next to them with five children between them. From the time they sat down in the sand until the time they left, these people never once stopped planning their vacation—while they were in the middle of it! Richard and his wife overheard them discussing where they were going to have dinner, how much fun they were going to have "tomorrow," how great it was going to be to watch the sunset "later on," as well as dozens of other future-oriented plans.

In the meantime, the five children had built, played in, and eventually destroyed one of the most incredible sand structures Richard had ever seen. They had so much fun and laughed so hard that he thought they might need to be carried away. He and his wife enjoyed watching them almost as much as they enjoyed watching their own children. Sadly, all four parents missed the entire show. All the moments had come and gone. They were so busy planning how much fun they were *going* to have that they forgot to actually have fun! One of our favorite quotes sums up this all-too-common scenario: "Life is what's happening while we're busy making other plans."

Obviously, there is a time for planning and there is a time for not paying attention to your children. But that day on the beach in Hawaii was neither of those times. And most of us do on a regular basis what these two couples were doing. Our years with our children slowly slip away while we are busy making other plans. Rather than listening to our children, our mind is somewhere else, busy planning a more enjoyable event. Rather than embracing our infant, we're busy longing for the day we have more time for ourselves. Rather than enjoying our family dinner together tonight, we're busy planning for a better time next week at the restaurant. Rather than living in the flow, enjoying each step along the way, we spend too much time in process mode, planning our life, which will begin later. Planning, planning, always planning. Someday is always going to be better than today—or so we believe.

We've seen parents so insistent on taking good photographs of some special event with their children that they miss the real event. We've seen parents miss their child's first steps because they were busy taking pictures, only the camera wasn't working, and we've seen parents miss much of their only daughter's wedding doing the very same thing with a video camera. There is a common belief that we'll look at the pictures later, and then we'll really enjoy the event. Meanwhile, it's all happening right here, right now.

Ideally, we can become more conscious of the beauty of the here and now; we can slow down to the speed of life enough to recognize that life is happening right now, in this moment. As you improve your ability to keep your attention in this moment, you will enjoy far more of life's special moments with your children.

5. YOU LOSE SIGHT OF YOUR COMPASSION

A calm mind, operating at the speed of life, is a compassionate mind. A speeded-up mind is a mind thinking too quickly, often losing perspective and compassion.

It's difficult to be a child—whether an infant or a teenager. Each age has its unique challenges, and each age has its own set of limitations. When your mind is moving too quickly, you can easily lose sight of this fact. When things aren't going well or when behavior isn't perfect, you will tend to react too harshly, without compassion. Because you are easily annoyed and are thinking things through too quickly, you'll blame your child for things when no blame is needed. Rather than remembering that children often learn through conflict and having compassion for how difficult it must be to be in so much conflict, you'll overreact and accuse your child of being "too angry" or "too frustrated."

When your mind slows down, when you're in healthy psychological functioning, it's easy to stay compassionate. Your perspective is larger. You remember your own child-hood and how frustrating it sometimes was. Your heart stays open, even in the midst of chaos, which sets as good an example as is possible. This, in turn, helps your children trust that you are there for them, even during those times when they are acting a little crazy. In the long run, they'll love you for it.

6. YOU EXPECT TOO MUCH FROM YOUR CHILDREN

One of the major problems associated with a busy mind in the parenting years is that a speeded-up mind—a mind that takes its thoughts too seriously—often expects too much from other people, particularly children. This is easy to understand when you consider how easily irritated you can become when you have too much on your mind or when you're too busy. Very simply, when you're irritated you have little tolerance; you expect near-perfect behavior and near-perfect performance. When you don't get these, you're an-noyed, bothered. And, if you're like most people, you let others know about your dissatisfaction.

When you expect too much from your children, they feel it, either directly or intuitively. They feel unappreciated, as if they aren't good enough, an experience that often results in low self-esteem and even deviant behavior.

When you slow down to the speed of life, you'll immediately notice how much more tolerance you have for your children and how much more accepting you become. You'll expect less and appreciate more. A mind operating at the speed of life accepts things—and people—for what they are, right now. You'll still encourage your children to be their very best, but you won't demand that they be better than they are to earn your love. The result will be that your children will feel more loved and respected, which will increase their feeling of self-worth.

In short, when we slow down to the speed of life and learn to live in the present moment, we can eliminate most of the anxiety associated with raising children.

Slowing down allows you to gain access to your healthy psychological functioning, which helps you keep things in perspective—the good and the bad, the easy and the difficult, the joys and the sorrows. You'll take it all in stride, while at the same time having even more passion and zest for life. When you do lose it, slowing down to the speed of life will help you quickly regain your perspective with ease and grace.

One of the key benefits of mental health is the peace you feel. When you feel good—when you have what you want in an emotional sense—life is much easier to digest; things (including your children) don't have to be perfect in order for you to be happy. The same issues that can bend you out of shape, frustrate you, and annoy you when you have a speeded-up mind can be approached with greater perspective and wisdom when approached in a calmer, healthier mind-set.

THE BENEFITS OF SLOWING DOWN

Now that we have reviewed some of the problems that exist in parenting because of a speeded-up mind, let's discuss what happens to you, as a parent, when you slow down to the speed of life. We've identified seven primary benefits of slowing down.

1. *Your day-to-day experience will be heightened. Ordinary moments will become quite beautiful.* Slowing down to the speed of life allows you to appreciate ordinary moments as if they were extraordinary. A mind that is fully in the moment is able to see, hear, and experience life's moments in a whole new way, with heightened awareness. Aspects of life that you used to take for granted you can now see with a keener, more respectful eye. You become able to appreciate the magic and incredible miracle of life, perhaps for the first time. As Richard's mind has slowed down, for example, he has noticed that his need for special activities has diminished. Rather than waiting for a weekend at the beach to have fun with his kids, he's found that sitting together on the stairs talking or sitting outside and watching the day go by has essentially the same value. The more relaxed he has become, the more he enjoys his ordinary, everyday moments.

As you appreciate the miracle of parenting, many of the things you used to get upset about will seem insignificant in your mind. Just as a person who discovers she has six months to live begins to appreciate life like never before, so a person who slows down to the speed of life and gains access to healthy functioning begins to see that much of what upsets us as parents doesn't really matter very much. And when you're not so busy being upset, your energy and attention are focused on the beauty of life and the joy of sharing it with your children.

2. *You'll become less reactive and more responsive.* Constant hurry and rush take their toll on your nervous system. A mind that is moving too quickly loses control over itself, and responsive thinking is replaced by an ongoing series of reactions. With a speeded-up mind, you are less able to recognize when you become caught up in thoughts about your children. As you slow down to the speed of life, however, you'll notice that your thinking will shift to a more reflective state. Peace and responsiveness toward your children will replace reactions. Using the baseball analogy, the ball will appear to be coming at you in slow motion as opposed to being shot out of a gun, and your responses to the challenges of parenting will likewise be more measured and sure.

3. *Your loving feelings and your appreciation for the gift of being a parent will increase.* We've already discussed how a speeded-up mind encourages you to miss the good times with your children. In a similar way, when your mind is moving too quickly, it's not available to receive many of the loving feelings that can accompany parenting. Very simply, the mind is too busy moving in other directions; it's everywhere but right here! As you slow down to the speed of life, however, your mind is in a more receptive state. This allows you to appreciate the joy of parenting and provides the space in which to feel grateful.

Gratitude is a natural feeling that is present when the mind isn't distracted by thoughts of overwhelm and distress. The more oriented toward the present moment you become— the more you slow down your thinking—the more gratitude you will feel.

4. *You will model peaceful, slowed-down behavior.* How does it look to your children—what silent messages are you sending them—when you frantically rush around the house reminding them what a hurry they should be in? We've actually seen parents yelling out in frustration for their kids to relax and calm down! Unfortunately, children model our frenzied behavior. If we yell, they will too. As you slow down to the speed of life, you will notice something quite remarkable: Your kids will slow down too.

As we calm down, we provide the environment for others to do the same. Usually, if we can gain access to our mental health, clear our mind, and relax, our kids will feel our sense of calm and will begin to calm down too. Richard was once in a horrible traffic jam with his two young children in the car. All around him, he could see frustrated parents in the same boat. In all cases, when the parent looked frustrated, the kids looked visibly shaken. Noticing the other parents helped Richard to experience thought recognition, which created a shift in his own thinking. He calmed down to the point of being totally relaxed. He put some very soothing music on the radio to replace the news. Almost instantly, and like magic, both his children also relaxed. The younger one fell fast asleep on the lap of the older child. A potentially frustrating situation had turned into a very pleasant experience.

5. *You'll eliminate potential regrets about not having been there for your kids.* When you're truly present for your children—when your mind isn't preoccupied with the distractions of day-to-day life and you are able to focus your attention in the present moment—you won't have to worry that your kids will look back on their childhood and say, "My dad (or mom) wasn't there for me." Children often feel

this way not because their parents were physically absent (although this may have been true), but because their parents were psychologically absent. Mom and Dad were thinking about what had happened that morning and what would happen that night and everything that they had to do in between.

Children, even more than adults, feel this psychological distance, this lack of being truly present. It feels to them that we're not interested in them—that there isn't enough time and that they aren't as important as everything else.

Being there for your children does not necessarily mean spending more time with them, but being more present with them when you are together. As you become more present, which happens naturally when you slow down to the speed of life, you will find that both you and your children will feel more satisfied, as though you've had enough quality time together. Life is a series of moments, one after another. If you are present, one moment at a time, then when "someday" arrives, you will have no regrets—and neither will your children.

6. *Your wisdom will surface, and you'll know what actions to take and what decisions to make to raise your kids to their full potential.* One of the fears that many people have about slowing down is that they will get too relaxed or lazy; they won't push their kids hard enough or won't help their kids reach their full potential. Actually, the opposite is true. As you slow down, your wisdom will surface and will provide you with needed answers. When you're speeded up, you will tend to repeat mistakes and make rash, habitual decisions. As your mind slows down, however, new, creative answers and decisions will replace habitual decisions and ways of doing things. You will notice that as you spend time with your children while you are engaged in free-flowing thinking, you will see

beyond their present behaviors and shortcomings to the human potential that lies within them. Seeing their innate potential seems to draw out the innate mental health lying within them. Studies of resiliency in kids from dysfunctional homes who turned out healthy showed one common denominator among the children: Some significant adult in their life believed in them and saw their potential. Never give up on the power of innate mental health in your children.

7. *You'll stop thinking that parenting is so hard.* When your mind is in a rush—when you pay too much attention to the thoughts that are racing through it—you will sense an enormous amount of stress. There will be too much to keep track of and too much on your mind. When your thinking is too active, parenting can seem like driving in a traffic jam: Everywhere you look there is chaos and confusion. Little things will get to you. In short, parenting will seem difficult.

When you slow down to the speed of life, however, everything becomes clearer, including answers to difficult issues. Instead of feeling like you are driving in a traffic jam, you will feel like you are driving alone on a country road. Life will seem to come at you at a slower pace, giving you more time to respond and to see the bigger picture. In short, being a parent will seem easier.

STRATEGIES FOR SLOWING DOWN TO THE SPEED OF LIFE

There are seven proven strategies to slowing down and becoming a more relaxed, effective, and loving parent. By implementing each of these strategies in your life, you will take valuable steps toward your goal of slowing down to the speed of life.

1. Become More Oriented to the Present Moment

One of the primary keys to effective, joyful parenting is the same as the key to slowing down to the speed of life: Learn to live more of your life in this moment. So much of the time we are reviewing some aspect of our experience that is over and done with—this morning's quarrels between siblings, last semester's poor report card, last night's disrespectful comments. Or we are rehearsing an unknown or feared future—What if my child doesn't get into college? What will happen if the kids can't get along on our vacation? What if Sara can't meet any new friends? All of these concerns (and thousands of others like them), past and future, are just thoughts.

Consider this:

Imagine your life as a time line.

You are born————right now————the moment you die.

Consider everything that has ever happened to you in your life as it exists right now—pleasant experiences, embarrassing moments, moments of passion and sadness, grief, success, failure. At this moment in your life, looking back, what realm is everything in? Is it actual reality or merely thoughts in your mind? If you guessed that it's in the realm of thought, you're right. If you fainted in a public speaking class (as Richard did in high school), it's no longer real, it's only a memory. If you were a high school cheerleader thirty years ago, it's now only a thought. Anything and everything that has ever happened in your life exists now only in memory.

Now consider the future. Everything that ever will happen to you in the future is, in this moment, only a thought. It hasn't yet happened. You can't touch it; you can only anticipate it, think about it. You may become rich and famous or broke and homeless, but whatever may happen, at this moment it's all thought.

That leaves you with this moment and this moment alone! This present moment is the only "real" moment that exists in real time—right now. But remember, this moment too is constantly changing and it too is experienced through thought. The moment vanishes and is replaced by the next one and so forth.

This exercise helps to emphasize how precious this moment really is by reminding you that all other moments are only an illusion. This moment is the only real one there is. Appreciate each new moment instead of focusing on moments that are over or yet to be, and you will operate at the speed of life. As you do, your experience of parenting will be transformed. Remember, a mind that isn't distracted with its own thoughts about the past or future is able to make wise, appropriate decisions.

Let us emphasize that it's possible that your child will indeed have difficulty meeting new friends (future concern) or that he did get into some type of trouble (past fact). However, that doesn't change the fact that right here, right now, all past and future concerns are only thoughts in your mind. This is not a prescription for denial, for pretending that life is different than it really is. Instead, it's a reality check, a reminder that the only true working unit of your life is this very moment. The rest is all in your imagination.

CONSIDER THE POSSIBILITY

Clear your mind of as many thoughts as you can, and be here—in this moment. Take a few deep breaths and relax. Bring to mind a concern that you have about something that you didn't approve of that happened to one of your children. Maybe he got into trouble, or maybe she didn't do well on a test. Notice that your concern is brought to life via your own thinking. Now bring yourself back to this moment and recognize that whatever your concern was, it's now true only in the realm of thought. It's no longer real; it's only a thought.

Now do the same thing with a future-oriented concern, such as, Will your child be able to make friends at her new school? Again, notice that your concern, in this present moment, is only a thought. As you bring your attention back to this moment, you'll become aware that your concern is only a thought. The only real moment is right now. This understanding frees you from the bondage of the past and the fear of the future. It helps you slow down to the speed of life by keeping your attention on the only moment that you have any control over— this one.

Finally, with regard to living in the present moment, don't make the mistake, as many do, of mystifying the experience or making it too complicated. Experiencing the present moment is nothing more than seeing life in free-flowing mode instead of from the memory. That's all. With your attention in the here and now, you will slow down to the speed of life.

2. Learn to Accept Each Moment as It Arises

Tap into the beauty and uniqueness of this moment instead of anticipating how wonderful the next one is going to be or remembering how special a past moment was.

Each moment is new and unique. You've never had this moment before, and you never will again. As you tap into the beauty of your constantly changing moments by becoming more oriented to the present one, you'll find yourself struggling with your moments far less and replacing your judgments with love and appreciation.

Rather than judging each moment as good ("I like this one") or bad ("I don't like this one"), see if, instead, you can accept your moments as they come to you by remaining in the free-flowing mode. And when you notice yourself slipping out of free-flowing mode (thought recognition), you'll find that your thinking is making appropriate shifts. You may be confronted with a new challenge or obstacle, or you may have an opportunity to learn something new.

One thing is for certain: As a parent, you will someday—perhaps sooner than you expect—look back on your experience and wonder, "Why did I make such a big deal out of that?" By accepting each moment as it arises, you'll eliminate a great deal of your future regret.

Let us share a funny story about being touched—or not touched, as the case may be—by ordinary life. A couple we know was vacationing in Hawaii, standing on a beach watching a beautiful sunset, hardly able to believe how magnificent the sight was. A woman approached them and overheard the wife say, "I can't believe how beautiful this is." While walking away from the spectacular display of beauty, the woman replied, "You should have seen the sunset in Tahiti."

When your attention isn't on the moment at hand but on something else, you'll tend to compare even good experiences with others, as this traveler did, or you'll wonder about future experiences instead of enjoying the one you are having. As you learn to accept and appreciate each moment as it arises, parenting, as well as the rest of your life, will come alive again, providing the enjoyment and satisfaction it was meant to hold.

3. Keep Your Thought Attacks to a Minimum

Parenting is an aspect of life that changes very quickly, day to day, moment to moment. Often you have little or no warning when something alarming happens: Your child falls down and skins his knee, a fight between siblings breaks out, you get a disturbing phone call from the school office, you get yelled at for exerting authority, and so forth. Sometimes it seems like parenting is just one emergency after another after another. For this reason, parenting is a natural breeding ground for thought attacks.

Thought attacks occur most often when something goes wrong. Something unexpected happens, and almost instantly your mind takes over and embellishes the story. When

Richard's young daughters get into a fight, for example, his thoughts have the tendency to run with ideas like, "What am I doing wrong?"; "Kris [his wife] and I don't argue like this, where did they learn all this anger?" If he doesn't keep his thoughts in check by noticing them (thought recognition), he could easily allow his thinking to spiral out of control. But if he's fortunate enough to see what's happening, a shift will occur in his thinking, bringing with it inner peace.

When your mind is still and your environment is calm, parenting is easy and rewarding. But when things get chaotic, out of hand, and out of your control, problems start and your mind is likely to speed up. This is when it's essential to keep your thought attacks under control. Recognize your thinking early, an appropriate shift will occur, and all will be well.

CONSIDER THE POSSIBILITY

Imagine that you are at a frightening movie about human-eating sharks. Did you bring a harpoon to the theater? Of course not! The reason you can watch a scary movie, eat popcorn and candy, then walk out of the theater with a minimum amount of fear is that you know that "it's just a movie."

Your thinking is much like a movie. In fact, your thinking is to your personal reality as the clips of film are to what you see up on the screen. In both cases, what you are experiencing seems real, but in neither case is it actually real. In the case of the movie, it's just film being projected onto the screen. In the case of your thoughts, it's just your thoughts. Your thoughts have no power to hurt you without your consent—without *you* taking them too seriously.

Keeping this perspective in mind works wonders when you are experiencing a thought attack, whether severe or mild. The next time your thinking is running wild because your teenager is out too late or your preschooler just picked a fight, take a deep breath and remind yourself that your thinking is just like a movie: It seems real, but it's still just your thinking. You'll probably find that you are either reviewing a painful or frustrating past experience or you are anticipating something that is yet to be. In most cases, you won't be in the present moment. If you can keep your thought attacks in check, you'll find that slowing down to the speed of life in parenting is a manageable endeavor.

---

4. Practice Early Thought Recognition

When you lose it, recognize that it was your thinking, not your child, that made you lose it. All parental thought attacks start out small and innocent. Something happens related to your child or children, and a thought comes to mind. Recently Richard was in New York on a business trip when he received an emergency phone call from his wife on the hotel voice mail. Something had happened to Kenna, his younger child.

Unfortunately, the voice mail cut off his wife's message, so most of the message was left to his imagination—and, boy, did he start to imagine! He knew Kenna was injured, but he had no idea how severely. His thoughts started spinning quickly. "Should I cancel my trip and go home? What happened? Whose fault was it?" Even the frightening question "Will she live?" somehow crept into his thinking. He was getting upset and frightened.

Fortunately, he woke up to the fact that he was thinking, engaged in a full-blown thought attack. He experienced a shift in the quality of his thinking and became aware that he was the thinker who was stuck in processing mode. This awareness saved his sanity as well as the rest of his trip. As he stepped back, he could watch his thinking: It was spinning, making up worst-case scenarios, embellishing even the worst possibilities. Almost immediately, the shift in his thinking calmed him down and brought him back to the present, which allowed his wisdom to surface.

In a calmer state of mind, he realized that had the injury been serious, his wife certainly would have had the front desk leave a message on his door. His wisdom returned. His calmer mind also gave him clues about who he could call to find out where his wife and daughter were. Fortunately, it turned out that the injury wasn't serious—only a badly sprained ankle. It was probably harder on his wife than it was on his daughter. After all, she was one who had to carry around forty-five pounds of frustrated child for the next three days!

Early thought recognition can save you from a great deal of parental frustration. The moment of genuine thought recognition is the moment you begin to slow down to the speed of life and to tap into a greater source of wisdom. Early thought recognition brings with it peace, serenity, and calmness. Remember, however, that thought recognition is something that happens on its own when you know of its importance. There's no need to try to achieve it or to walk around looking for thought recognition. It will begin to happen earlier and earlier simply because you know how important it is to slowing down to the speed of life.

5. *See Moods with Compassion*

In the previous chapter we found that when you are in a bad mood, little things can seem like really big deals, and big things can seem almost too much to handle. Problems seem impossible to solve, and they look like the tip of the iceberg. You have very little perspective, and, because you feel hopeless and negative, you tend to forget the joys of parenting. In low moods, you overreact and often offer unneeded and unwanted advice.

Yet, as we said earlier, because of the urgency you feel, it's during your low moods when your capacity is limited that you will try to make important decisions and solve pesky problems. You react to your negative feelings with negative thinking and behavior.

The same dynamic is true when your children are in low moods. They will say and do things in low moods that they would never say or do in a higher state of mind. In low moods, your children aren't going to like you; in higher moods, they will usually love you just the way you are. In lower moods they will look for and find your flaws, inconsistencies, and faults. In lower moods, your children will pick fights with each other and with you, and they will make poor decisions. They won't appreciate anything you do or have done for them. In fact, they will probably think of life as more of a burden.

Being compassionate toward moods, whether theirs or ours, is a powerful tool in parenting. It allows you to keep your perspective in everyday cases when most parents can't. When you're feeling low, angry, speeded up, trapped, or frustrated, being compassionate toward your mood allows you give yourself a break, cut yourself some slack. When you understand moods and have the humility to admit when you are in a bad mood, you make certain allowances for the way you are feeling. You say things like, "Of course I'm going to react like this right now—I'd better not trust my judgment." You learn to wait things out and not to take yourself and your reactions so seriously.

You keep the same perspective in mind when your children are low. You learn to give your kids a break—not to advocate or condone negative or disrespectful behavior, but simply to remember how distorted life looks in a low state of mind. You might, for example, brush off your son's comment, "You never play with me," or your daughter's complaint, "I'm the only girl in school who doesn't have her own telephone." A healthy respect for moods allows you to remember that in low moods your kids aren't making up those statements—that's really how life looks in that state of mind.

Understanding moods as a parent is like driving in a heavy downpour of rain knowing that your vision is impaired. You may have to keep driving, but you know that you must be careful.

RICHARD CARLSON AND JOSEPH BAILEY

CONSIDER THE POSSIBILITY

Picture yourself in a really bad mood. Imagine you're hurried, annoyed, and uptight. Now, think of two or three typical day-to-day events pertaining to your role as a parent. Here are a few examples: You walk into a room that looks like the city dump, you notice the size of the laundry pile is taller than you are, someone tracks mud all over your carpet, your hear the kids fighting like cats and dogs over some little thing.

In a horrible mood, how do those things seem to you? In all likelihood, if you're honest, you'll say, "Awful."

Now, imagine those exact same events, only this time you're in a philosophical, good mood. Certainly you'd rather not have to deal with these types of things—who does? But if you're in a good mood, you find it easier to take daily life in stride. It's not that you like everything you have to do, but, on the other hand, things aren't that big of a deal, either. You simply do what you have to do and move on. In higher moods, you don't think about things as much; you simply do what's before you.

If you are in a low mood, don't take your thinking too seriously. Don't try to figure out what's wrong with your life or what's wrong with your children. If you do, you'll just frustrate yourself. A better solution when you are in a low mood is to clear your mind to the best of your ability and let go. As your mood rises, solutions and answers will enter your mind just as surely as the problems do in a more negative state. Remember, your mood may be low, but that doesn't mean your life is a failure!

---

6. Practice Doing One Thing at a Time

One of the most frustrating aspects of parenting is the stress that is created by trying to do too many things at once. It is good to practice doing one thing at a time whenever possible. Doing one thing at a time helps you develop calm yet impeccable concentration. A mind that is able to stay focused on what it is doing is a mind that is engaged in the present moment. And in the present moment, when we are aware of our thinking, thought attacks don't happen. In order to have a thought attack about anger, fear, or overwhelm, your in-the-moment concentration must be broken, and your mind must wander to the past or future.

Richard remembers a time when both his girls had friends over at the house. Although the house was chaotic, he chose that particular time to try to organize a closet. He spread stuff all over the family room floor at the same time he was being asked to make lunch, find this and that, answer the phone, accept deliveries at the door, and clean the kitchen. He felt completely scattered, jumping from one thing to the next, never quite finishing what he set out to do. After about an hour, he thought he was going to go crazy. Fortunately, he experienced thought recognition—he noticed his thinking was speeded up, out of control. This led to a shift in his thinking to a slower, calmer type of thinking—his free-flowing mode. This helped him to remember the wisdom of doing one thing at a time. He decided to leave the mess on the floor (something that is difficult for him to do) until everything calmed down. When it finally did, he took the phone off the hook and stayed focused on his closet project. Within a half hour, it was all done. What a relief!

The deeper aspect of doing one thing at a time is to keep our attention focused on only one thing at a time. Often our thinking is like a roller-coaster. We're up here, down there, and all over the place—spinning quickly. When this happens, we're not in the present moment but everywhere else. Because our thoughts are also feelings, this scattered thinking becomes tension, agitation, and stress. A calmer, one-pointed mind can be cultivated, however, by learning to give undivided attention to whatever we are doing at the moment. This simple understanding prevents tension from developing because our mind is at rest instead of jumping on every train of thought that comes along.

7. Live in the Free-Flowing Mode as Much as Possible

As we have discussed, creative thinking is essential to all personal growth, change, development, and evolution. It is also essential for a peaceful experience of parenting. When we learn to live in the free-flowing mode of thinking most of the time and to reserve the processing mode for tasks that require planning, calculating, and analyzing, our life and experience of parenting become much easier and more manageable. We begin to live in the deeper feelings that come with flow thinking—gratitude, joy, relaxation, compassion, and a sense of ease.

While in the free-flowing mode, our thinking is responsive, appropriate to the present experience that is before us. We are not responding out of past habits or beliefs but are dealing with the situation in a creative, appropriate manner.

The mistake that many parents make is being too much "in their heads" when dealing with their children. The effort is futile, since, as you probably know, you can't figure out your children. Trying to do so only leads to frustration and confusion. Even if you could figure them out, by the time you did so, they would have changed again. It's far more effective to stay in a reflective state of mind, which allows you to adjust to the constant changes and challenges you face.

As parents, we are always dealing with children who are changing, growing, and evolving. What was appropriate last year is certainly not appropriate now. Life is constantly changing, and we must flow with the changes. To know what is an appropriate response, you cannot look to your memory for the answer. Instead, you will find the right course by letting go of your analytical thinking, clearing your mind, and waiting patiently for an answer from your wisdom. This wisdom can come only from the free-flowing mode.

We explained earlier that clearing your mind is much like letting the silt settle in water. You simply do nothing, and the silt automatically settles on its own. Anything you do to try to settle the silt actually keeps it stirred up. This is why you can't try to relax. Relaxing is a natural by-product of the free-flowing mode.

The free-flowing mode of thinking will automatically start feeding you a flow of thoughts that will give you the answers you need and will help you slow down to the speed of life, enabling you to be calmer and wiser. Trust in the free-flowing mode, and your experience of parenting will be transformed.

SUMMARY

Contrary to popular belief, parenting can be a joyful experience, without the hurry, rush, and stress experienced by so many people. The key, as in virtually all areas of life, is to slow down to the speed of life. If we can learn to gain access to our healthy psychological functioning, we will make wise decisions that are appropriate to the situation at hand. We will also enjoy the beautiful gift of raising children.

CHAPTER 7

Working Smarter

I have a microwave fireplace. You can lay in front of it all night in only eight minutes.
COMEDIAN STEPHEN WRIGHT

Many people attribute the hectic rhythm of their lives to the fast-paced nature of their work. The increased demands on people's time in an era of downsizing, cost cutting, international competition, and increased technology has left workers feeling insecure, stressed, and overwhelmed with more to do in less time. When changes are made, the human factor is often the last to be considered People are working longer hours, with more intensity, but are they working smarter? Is the efficiency level going up or down? Are workers satisfied with their jobs? Do employers care so much about their stockholders and the bottom line that they forget about their employees? Are employees really happy with their work lives?

In this chapter we will address how slowing down to the speed of life applies to the world of work. We will discuss how slowing down to the moment increases our ability to manage people while keeping the human factor in mind. It also helps us relate to others, make intelligent decisions, be motivated and productive, decrease stress, manage our time at a sane pace, use our creative thinking to meet new challenges, and gain access to our common sense in times of crisis and change.

Ironically, you need to slow down in order to deal with increased demands. When people are feeling rushed and frantic, they make more mistakes, deal with others poorly, burn out, and lose their ability to think clearly, creatively, and intelligently. All you need to do is visit an organization that is speeded up—that works at a frantic pace—and you'll see poor decisions being made, low morale, employees stealing from the company, individuals sneaking out of work, and dysfunctional meetings where virtually no one can agree on a direction.

In order to work smarter, workers need to slow down to the speed of life—to learn to be more in the moment. Due to the avalanche of information and the speed with which we receive it, we need to learn to use our thought process in a way that is more intelligent—one that doesn't stress us out. This is what we have been calling healthy psychological functioning. To put it more boldly, we believe that the psychological health of companies will be a major competitive edge in these times of global economic evolution. Companies that are operating in healthy psychological functioning will make better decisions, be more farsighted, have happier and thus more loyal and motivated employees, and experience less illness and absenteeism and fewer accidents. Employees operating at the speed of life are smart, productive, and cooperative. The human factor is the cutting edge of competition.

WORKING SMARTER, NOT HARDER

Regardless of our profession, the more often we are functioning in a healthy psychological way, the more we will use our common sense and the more job satisfaction we will experience. When Joe recently asked a physician how she'd like to improve psychologically on the job, she said, "I'd like to make all patients feel as though I had all the time in the world to devote to them. The reality is, the HMO is demanding that I see more patients per hour, and I don't feel I have enough time to see them all due to meetings and paperwork." If she learned to live in healthy psychological functioning, she would be able to switch back and forth at ease from processing thinking to free-flowing thinking, so she would have a bedside manner with all her patients, even in her fast-paced world.

Working smarter instead of harder requires understanding how to keep our bearings and live in the moment. Take John, for example. He was just told that his department needed to downsize and that he would temporarily be doing both his job and the job of his co-worker, who had been laid off. John's first reaction was to feel angry ("It's not fair!"), then overwhelmed ("They are asking me to do the impossible!"), and finally insecure ("How am I ever going to be able to do this? What if they replace me too and I'm out of a job?"). If John had understood the principles of healthy functioning, he would have recognized by his feelings that he had started using unhealthy analytical thinking. He would have regained his bearings and realized that he needed a fresh perspective to deal with his job in a creative manner. He would trust that if he didn't see a solution right now, he could put it on the back burner and his creative intelligence would come up with a great solution. He would see that the number one priority during times of change is not to lose his bearings and his perspective. He would trust that if he had his mental health, he would be in the best possible position to see his way through a very difficult situation. Furthermore, if his boss had understood about the human factor better, he would have known how to present this difficult decision to the employees in a way that would have minimized insecurity and resulting inefficiency. Or if the boss had anticipated the situation sooner, he might have been able to avoid it altogether. Obviously, when an entire company is operating from a mentally healthy state, there is a positive effect on decision making at all levels.

Working smart implies listening, reflecting, and then acting rather than reacting out of habit. It means having ultimate confidence in your instincts to do the right thing in the moment, when you don't have time to sort through things. Working smart means drawing on your memory and experience in a way that helps you in the moment instead of blinding you by past experience. It means being able to be in rapport with others, knowing that without rapport you can't have teamwork and communication. It means knowing how to live your life in the moment—doing one thing at a time, with presence and at a pace that lead to balance in your personal and work life.

RAISING THE BOTTOM LINE
BY LIVING ABOVE IT

Visionary
Dynamic
Self-Motivated

Stressed
Survival Oriented
Bureaucratic/Dysfunctional

Living above the line means living at the level of understanding that is able to recognize thinking in the moment—whether we are operating in an free-flowing mode or are trapped in analytical thinking, unable to recognize when it's time to let go. As our level of understanding gradually grows through recognizing our thinking more and more often, our life—including our work life—improves in every respect. Managers tend to become more inspired and responsive to people and changing times. Workers are generally more creative, cooperative, productive, and satisfied with their jobs.

Different habits, values, and behaviors accompany each level of understanding in the above diagram. It is interesting to note that organizations tend to hire and keep employees at their same level of understanding; people are more comfortable with people who think like they do. The level of understanding at which an organization operates determines its culture, productivity level, employee attitudes, and ultimately its bottom line—its financial success (in the case of a business) or the success of its clients (in the case of service and educational organizations). Let's take a look at how organizations at each level of understanding operate.

In organizations at the lowest level of understanding, which we have called the Bureaucratic/Dysfunctional level, the thinking of most employees is self-absorbed and fearful and is often blinded by tunnel vision. Workers tend to feel overwhelmed, hurried, and out of control. They are totally exhausted, agitated, defensive, and prone to arguments and anger. Companies at this level are full of cliques, gossip, bad-mouthing of the company, disrespect, and sabotage of company efforts. Bureaucracies that have lost their vision decades ago, groups that are highly political, or companies that have become polarized between management and labor are examples of this type of organization. Organizations below this level of functioning are either bankrupted or in anarchy.

In companies at a slightly higher level of understanding, employees' thinking is oriented toward survival. Workers tend to feel negative—full of blame, worry, and resentments. They are irritable and rushed, and they experience no sense of teamwork; they often feel burned out, defensive, and angry. Organizations at this level have extremely high turnover rates and make many costly mistakes, and employees as well as managers frequently blame others and point the finger at outside factors or each other to explain their lack of success or productivity. There is a high rate of accidents, illness, and absenteeism in Survival-Oriented companies. The difference between a company at this level and at the lowest one is that this company is able to function well enough to get the basic job done.

As we go up the scale, we find an organization operating at the Stressed level. Thinking here is less negative but still is not clear and creative. People tend to be busy-minded, distracted, stressed, and working hard but not smart. They are able to cope with their level of stress through mechanisms such as gallows humor, office pranks, and a high level of competition among workers. These organizations tend to put in long hours but have a lot of unproductive waste, many errors, and low productivity. Employees burn out and take sick leave as a way of surviving the pressure. In spite of all this, these companies are often financially quite successful.

We are now moving up the scale to an organization whose workers are generally living above the line. We call this the Self-Motivated level of operation. Even under pressure, the thinking of these workers tends to be clear and full of common sense. They are satisfied with their jobs, comfortable, productive, and self-motivated, so they don't need much active management. They spend their time efficiently and see solutions to problems more readily. They work as a team supporting one another and being cooperative toward achieving the company's goals and vision.

Moving farther up the scale, we see workers at the Dynamic level. Thinking has become more instinctual, intuitive, and responsive. Employees of this organization operate in free-flowing mode most of the time. The leaders are in service to the employees; they are positive and supportive. The employees are energized and are usually two steps ahead of the customer or changing times. They listen well to one another and leapfrog one another with their creativity. Meetings are dynamic, creative, fun, and less necessary than at lower levels. There is a high rate of job satisfaction and enjoyment in this level of organization.

At the highest level of understanding, which we call the Visionary level, organizational thinking is very creative and original. There is a steady flow of new ideas, accompanied by practical thinking to implement them. Leadership is exhilarated and visionary, and the company sets new standards in its industry. These are highly successful organizations, and people feel extremely fortunate to be able to work in them. These groups operate with a vision of service to others; they try to extend help beyond their own employees to the community as a whole. They are making the world a better place.

It is apparent that the higher the level of understanding, the more successful and enjoyable an organization will be. Instead of trying to force change from the outside in, realizing that change will occur automatically as individuals and groups gain more psychological wisdom induces change from the inside out. Organizations living below the line are looking to outside solutions or factors to blame, whereas groups above the line are tapping into their common sense and free-flowing thought to *create* a better work system.

Now let's look at some of the common issues in organizations and how to approach them in a healthy manner. The following factors help us realize our full potential at work :

- Pacing: The Tortoise Approach to Time Management
- Work Relationships (Rapport, Presence, Conflict, Boundaries, Dealing with Difficult People, Moods, Giving Feedback)
- Meetings: Getting in the Way of Work or Helping You Get the Job Done?
- Making Decisions
- Dealing with Deadlines

PACING: THE TORTOISE APPROACH
TO TIME MANAGEMENT

Remember the story of the tortoise and the hare? The hare started out fast, leaving the tortoise far behind. He soon became exhausted and had to take a nap, overconfident that he would outrun his slower competitor. The tortoise paced himself, plodding along but never stopping. The tortoise won the race.

Many of us say we don't have adequate time to complete all the things our job demands, much less get it all done and still have time for family, friends, and fun. To try to cope with the pace of our work life, we often turn to technology (electronic organizers, laptop computers, pagers, cellular phones, fax machines, e-mail, the Internet) and time management systems. Ironically, the more time we save through time-saving devices, the more we try to cram into a day. We just keep raising our expectations of ourselves, our employees, and our families. This innocent attempt to find more time is doomed to fail because we are failing to recognize where our experience of time comes from—thought. Slowing down our thinking process can help us pace ourselves at work so that we manage our work time differently.

The experience of time has very little to do with clock time and everything to do with thought. Do you experience time differently when you are waiting for someone who is late than when you are the one who is late? In the first case time goes slow, in the second time goes fast. Our perception of time is directly related to how we are thinking. The root canal patient's time drags on painfully slowly, while the dentist's day flies by with not enough time to see every patient.

What we are thinking determines how impatient we feel, how anxious we are about the future, and how frustrated we become with how slowly things are happening. If you don't think time is related to thinking, travel to a country where people experience time differently than do North Americans. We are likely to feel stressed, impatient, and angry, while they are relaxed and puzzled as to why we are so upset and in a hurry.

Our experience of anxiety and stress comes from being out of the moment and engaged in unhealthy analytical thinking. When we get caught up in our thinking, we try to do two or three things at once, we are highly distracted with thoughts of the past or the future, and we usually don't do very well the task that is right in front of us. If we could learn to value the free-flowing mode of thinking—having faith in the process of living from moment to moment, calmly doing one thing at a time—we would find that we would make fewer mistakes, experience more enjoyment and satisfaction, and actually get more done! You are always living in this moment; will you live it present or absent? Will you live in a speeded-up state of mind or a calm one? If you are in flow or free-flowing thinking, it will seem as though you have plenty of time, even if you are on tight deadlines and have a great deal of responsibility. Slowing down to the comfortable pace of a tortoise happens when we recognize our thinking and bring ourselves back to the moment— living above the line.

To our surprise, as the two of us have learned to live more in the moment, above the line, whether it is at our work or at home, we have found that although we have the experience or feeling of time slowing down, the truth is that at the end of the day we have accomplished more than we used to when we felt rushed and frantic. Below the line, we used to spend an enormous amount of time getting organized and reorganized, procrastinating, making mistakes, and doing unimportant busywork. In addition, we had a difficult time delegating tasks to others who were far better than we at doing them, either because we didn't want to let go of control or because it just seemed easier to do them ourselves. The more we thought of all we had to do, the more overwhelmed and fatigued we became and the less we accomplished.

When we get caught up in process-oriented thinking about the future, we run what we have to do over and over in our heads while doing some other task, and we become fatigued. So much of the fatigue in stress comes not from the actual work, but from thinking about all we have to do. Further, as employees, we spend much of our day talking about all we have to do or have been doing. "I can't believe how stressed I've been—there's so much to do!" Have you ever had the experience of lying in bed in the morning, going over the day ahead, and feeling totally exhausted before you even got up? This unnecessary thinking robs us of rest, enjoyment, and the feeling of ease. If we can recognize our thinking in the moment, we can bring ourselves back to healthy psychological functioning and with it have access to a more intelligent mode of thinking that has the best time management system built into it—pacing.

Adequate pacing means never doing too much at a time. It's taking time to reflect, set priorities, and listen. The old carpenter's adage, "Measure twice, cut once," sums up the philosophy of pacing. It means retaining perspective and responding appropriately in the moment. Joe remembers building a log cabin with a friend many years ago. The friend was a skilled craftsman, but he seemed to work very slowly. Joe often felt impatient with him, but as time went on he learned to see the wisdom in the friend's slowness. This man took time to reflect on what he was doing until he came up with the best possible way to do a particular task. In addition, he rarely had to redo a task, and he rarely wasted any materials; thus his costs remained low. In addition, Joe and his friend really enjoyed working together. Joe had no idea, at the time, why he enjoyed that building project so much, but it now seems obvious. The two of them were working in the moment. Ironically, Joe's friend completed the whole job as fast as, if not faster than, most carpenters could have.

When we pace ourselves, we use our resources wisely, we change according to what is necessary in the moment, and we see how to elicit the cooperation of others. When we slow down to the speed of life—to tortoise speed—our reward will be calmness, happiness, productivity, and a successful life. We too will win the race.

WORK RELATIONSHIPS

With noticeably few exceptions, most of us spend at least a portion of our time working with other people. If our work relationships are not positive, they take away from productivity, efficiency, teamwork, and customer service. The basis of all healthy relationships is a feeling of respect, trust, warmth, goodwill, and lack of judgment. In a healthy relationship there is a feeling of being at ease. Living above the line, that is, recognizing that our experience of others is coming from our thinking, allows us to see the innocence of others and to take responsibility for our reactions to them.

Rapport

We call this feeling of being at ease "rapport." When we have rapport with others, we can do whatever we need to do at the moment—communicate about a new project, resolve a conflict, brainstorm a solution to a challenging situation. Rapport is the lubricant in virtually every social interaction. Lack of rapport becomes obvious in the negative feelings we or they begin to experience—tension, mistrust, anger, fear, discomfort, insecurity. When we lose rapport, we become serious, mechanical, and humorless. In addition, job satisfaction plummets, along with productivity. When we have rapport, we are present, lighthearted, and warm and respectful toward others.

When Joe was growing up, he worked at his dad's nursery. Two foremen there contrasted sharply in their rapport with others. Gus was stern, punctual to an extreme, distrustful of his workers, and unappreciative of the hard work that others did (he just expected it). Paul, on the other hand, was a model of hard work, pitching in whenever he was needed. Paul trusted others to do their jobs, and when mistakes were made, he patiently corrected his employees with a gentle hand.

Gus's crew made many mistakes and didn't show up for work consistently. When he wasn't physically present, nobody worked very hard, if at all, and the days seemed to drag on forever. In Paul's presence, everyone enjoyed their work, maintained a high level of productivity, and the days seemed to fly by.

The difference between Paul and Gus was the rapport that each had with his crew. Each was equally dedicated to his job, but Gus had a negative view of people—they were lazy, inferior, untrustworthy, and incompetent. Paul saw his crew members as wanting to do a good job and as people who were likable and fun to be with. He saw himself as one of them. Both foremen taught Joe the importance of rapport—one by practicing it, the other by lacking it.

Presence

Being oriented to the present moment is key to developing good rapport with our co-workers. Being present with another leads to good listening, excellent communication, and a feeling of connection or teamwork.

One of the rescue workers at the Oklahoma City bombing in 1995 was interviewed a year later about how his life was going. He became quite nostalgic about the time of the bombing and stated, "It may sound sick, but I miss the intensity of the time after the bombing. We were all working around the clock, but there was such a feeling of teamwork, purpose, and time just seemed to fly by. No one ever seemed to get tired." What he was describing is a level of enjoyment that occurs when people are present with one another, regardless of how terrible the circumstances. One of the most memorable moments of Joe's childhood was when his little town in eastern Minnesota flooded. Virtually everyone in the town stayed up all night in the cold, pouring rain. In one way or another, every man, woman, and child was involved in saving the town. People who were normally strangers worked together, becoming a highly effective team, striving together for a common goal.

We don't have to create a crisis in order to create the feeling of cooperation and shared purpose. They are the result of being present in the moment. When we are in the free-flowing mode, we are naturally present with others, and we bring that presence and intensity of the moment to our work relationships. Presence in relationships occurs when we are not distracted by a busy mind. Being present means really "being there" with our co-workers—whether in a meeting, on a break, or during a difficult discussion. Slowing down to the speed of life in work allows us to be present in relationships. As we move above the line in our understanding, our work relationships naturally become harmonious.

Conflict

Everyone sees life from a different perspective; we all create our experience of life through thinking. When we lose rapport, our differences can turn into conflict rather than enrichment.

Seeing life from different perspectives has the potential to enrich and expand all of our viewpoints, thus gaining for each of us a larger and deeper perspective. Seeing past our differences and listening to one another allow us to transcend our narrow viewpoint—to evolve, change, and grow. In the work environment, this means each member of the team contributes to the success of the organization by sharing his or her unique view.

Unfortunately, all too often our differences become the source of conflict, arguments, hostilities, and stalemate. People living below the line see differences as disagreement and as a threat to their power, authority, or perceived level of importance. When people are living above the line, they see differences as interesting, and they become curious about the other person's perspective.

Let's say an employee comes up with an idea that may save the company time and money in its inventory system. A supervisor who is living above the line would first listen to the employee nonjudgmentally and be open to the new idea, even if the idea had been tried before or if it didn't seem to have immediate value. Through this process the employee would feel respected, valued, and heard, even if the idea was ultimately rejected. The supervisor would ask questions in order to understand where the employee was coming from, thus ferreting out any potential good ideas. The employee might even be rewarded financially for any suggestions that lowered costs or increased profits. This is teamwork.

On the other hand, a supervisor who was living below the line would be threatened that someone else thought of the idea first. This supervisor might squelch the idea out of fear that it would make him or her look stupid or inferior to the employee. No listening would take place, thus discouraging employees from looking for ways of making the business more efficient, for when people don't feel valued, they turn off their creative intelligence.

Conflict can occur at many levels within an organization. The downfall of most partnerships is being unaware of how to deal with conflict. Just as in a marriage, when rapport disappears, differences come to the foreground and common interests fall to the background. When respect, trust, and rapport are lost, the lack of psychological health will lead to conflict, either overt or covert. This conflict can undermine the organization's success and even lead to its demise. Below the line, conflict is potentially a threat to the success of an organization; above the line, it is the potential source of its evolution, growth, and success.

There are five ways to deal with conflict effectively:

1. See differences as positive, interesting, enriching, and important to the creative process of running an organization.
2. If you are in conflict with a co-worker, follow the guidelines for having a heart-to-heart talk outlined in chapter 5. Move into your free-flowing mode, make sure the timing and mood are right, listen, and keep your rapport.
3. Look for areas of agreement rather than disagreement.
4. Keep the tone upbeat and positive; if this is not possible, leave the issue and come back to it later.
5. Stay above the line, and you will be able to come up with a hybrid solution that is better than all of the individual ideas combined. (We will talk more about this in the section on running meetings.)

Boundaries

An integral part of any organization's health is its ability to establish clear boundaries in responsibilities, roles, and levels of social appropriateness. Am I doing someone else's job? Is it appropriate to ask my co-worker to fill in for me on something that is normally my job? Is it okay to give the boss feedback on a particular issue? Did flirting with that person feel appropriate? These are all boundary questions. Scores of workshops are conducted on specific issues such as sexual harassment, racism, communication, and so forth, to deal with issues of boundaries.

When we are in free-flowing mode, these issues are easy to handle. We get a gut feeling when something is off in our relationships or is inappropriate. Trusting these feelings and acting on them protects us from crossing the boundary. For example, Sandra and Tom share a job in the accounts receivable division of a large company. They fill in for each other from time to time, but Sandra (who is feeling preoccupied with personal problems) starts to innocently take advantage of Tom's generous nature: Tom notices over time that he is doing a disproportionate share of the work. Instead of building resentment about this fact, however, he has a heart-to-heart talk with Sandra about it. She realizes that she has been doing less and less and apologizes to Tom, then makes an effort to do her share.

In a more difficult situation Gary (the supervisor) has Gail (his assistant) balance his personal checkbook on company time. Gary hates to do his checkbook and thinks it won't hurt anything because Gail isn't that busy. Gail feels in a bind. The task doesn't feel appropriate, but her boss is asking her to do it. She decides to put it on her back burner until her creative mode comes up with a solution. This mode takes into account all the variables—how important the task is, the timing of talking to her boss, how to bring it up, and so on. When the timing is right, she brings the issue up to her boss. Gary initially feels embarrassed and defensive, but in general he is operating above the line, so he takes her comments to heart and explores the possibility that what he is doing is out of line. The free-flowing mode is the radar that shows us how to maneuver around sensitive boundary issues.

In some conflicts one person is operating above the line and the other person isn't. What can you do then? In some cases it may be a good idea to bring in a third party, such as human resources or another co-worker. In other instances, you may need to wait until a situation calms down. In any case, your free-flowing mode will give you an appropriate answer to an inappropriate situation.

Dealing with Difficult People

When you are living above the line, in healthy functioning, dealing with difficult people is like going through a downpour with a good waterproof set of rainwear. Very little of the downpour gets to you—you are able to not take personally what the other person is saying or doing, even if it is directed at you. For example, if you have a co-worker who is operating below the line, acting in a way that is irritating to others, you may be able to see that person's innocence or even see the humor in the situation. One of us consulted with an organization where there was a person who most of the employees didn't like. She was paranoid, supercritical of everyone's performance, and always negative at staff meetings. She resisted virtually every new change in the company and was the one you could count on to drag her feet.

After receiving training in the concepts of living above the line, several of the other employees were able to see her in a new light. They began to see the difficulty she was going through relating to her health problems and personal issues. They were able to see that her behavior had nothing to do with them. This made them more tolerant of her negativity. As is often the case, she responded to their increased patience with less caustic actions. After a while, she began to recognize how difficult she had been, and she asked for her co-workers' support. Most of them responded positively.

Here are four suggestions for dealing with difficult people in the workplace:

1. See beyond their behavior to their human potential; then you will more likely elicit their healthy psychological functioning.
2. Give them the benefit of the doubt; they may be in a low mood or going through a difficult time.
3. See that it is in your best interest to be nonjudgmental and nonreactive; you are the one who has to live with your own feelings.
4. When in doubt about what to do, see if you are listening; remember that listening from the free-flowing mode will always give you the answer.

Moods

As we have said, moods are fluctuations in the quality of our thinking. Moods are a natural part of the human experience; they are our internal weather. Since we don't leave our psychological functioning at the doorstep when we enter the workplace, moods are very much a part of everyone's workday. When we learn to navigate our moods and everyone else's, we will experience much smoother sailing.

There are two key things to keep in mind about moods at work:

1. Recognize your own mood. By listening to your feelings as a compass, you will be able to tell when your mood has dropped. As we have said, almost always we will perceive outside circumstances as dictating our moods; the announcement of the deadline just before the holiday, the boss's outburst, or someone letting you down in a way that makes you late are all situations that we think cause our mood to shift. However, when we take responsibility for our own mood and the thinking that is causing it, we are moving in the direction of a change in our internal weather. We are also able to take our mood into account—to avoid, when possible, making important decisions in a low mood, to wait until our mood shifts before we call on that important customer, to wait until our mood is up before we ask for the raise (or time off). Recognizing our mood and acting accordingly is like dressing for the weather. Don't forget your umbrella!

2. Recognize other people's moods, and don't take them personally. When we start seeing people's moods, we begin to take them into account in the same way we listen to the weather report before we decide what to wear that day. This doesn't mean we change our own mood based on other people's moods; we simply take their mood into consideration. For example, if Sally sees that her secretary is unusually crabby today, she may wait until she is feeling better before scheduling her quarterly review. In a better mood, the secretary will be more receptive to her feedback; she will receive it more objectively and less defensively. Or if Jane, the secretary, sees that Sally is in a low mood, she may wait to tell her that she is pregnant and will be needing maternity leave during the busy season.

One of the biggest problems we have with other people's moods is when we take them personally. Many people assume they have caused the other person's low mood, and they immediately shift into unhealthy process mode—thinking about what it might have been that they did to cause it. Others become judgmental about someone's low mood and believe this gives them license to go into a low mood themselves. That would be like seeing a bus approaching and standing in the splashing range of a puddle; you are bound to get wet.

Don't try to figure out other people's moods; they're just part of life. Don't judge their low moods, since you probably have had one yourself in the past twenty-four hours. Most important, don't take their low mood personally, even if they are blaming you for it. You are responsible for your behavior, not for their thoughts about it. In other words, you are responsible for how you dress for the weather, but not for the weather itself.

CONSIDER THE POSSIBILITY

The next time you are with someone at work who is in a low mood, imagine that you are feeling the way this person does. How would you like to be treated by this person if your roles were reversed?

Giving Feedback

Many of us have occasion to give feedback to our fellow employees from time to time, whether it be through a formal review or through simply noticing—and pointing out—that someone forgot to do part of his or her job. As we discussed in the chapter on relationships, it is extremely important, when giving feedback, to make sure that rapport is in place and that you get permission. Asking for permission does two things: (1) It ensures that the other person will be ready to listen to you, and (2) it communicates respect. You may be thinking that you don't need the other's permission; after all, you may be the boss! That's like assuming that your mate can't wait for your feedback, just because she or he is your mate. You may have the *right* to give feedback, but unless the other person is actually listening, little if anything will be accomplished.

You may need to give feedback on something as minor as a missed a day of work or as major as telling someone he or she isn't suited for a particular job. The magnitude of the task dictates the amount of permission and rapport needed. If you get the proper rapport and permission, it's like anesthesia—you can perform major surgery with very little pain. Taking the few seconds it requires to get the rapport and permission you need can save days and weeks of mistakes or continued lack of productivity.

Let's take a situation and play it through two ways—below the line and above the line. The situation is that Joe, the manager, realizes that the report due today for his board meeting is not in his box. He was expecting Carmen, a supervisor, to have the report to him—on his desk—that morning. If Joe is operating below the line, he sees Carmen walking in the door of the plant and immediately confronts her about the late report: "Do you realize that I have to present to the board today? I'll look like a fool if I don't get that report before the meeting at two o'clock!" Carmen is caught off guard and immediately gets defensive and angry. She tries to explain that the computer is down, but Joe doesn't listen. Carmen, in turn, yells at Mary, her secretary, to get that report, which she is already working on, done by two o'clock. Mary, in turn, reacts with hurt and starts crying in front of a new customer, who is now wondering to himself, "What kind of a business is this, anyway?" All of this could have easily been avoided by taking a few seconds to gather some degree of rapport.

If Joe is living above the line, however, he realizes he doesn't have the report he needs for the meeting today. He sees Carmen walk in and asks if she has five minutes to talk. Carmen says that she is busy, but that if it's important she can talk. Joe calmly tells Carmen the situation and asks her (without assuming anything) to explain the status of the report as well as what's happening to solve the problem. Carmen lets him know that the computer was down yesterday but that she should easily be able to finish the report before two o'clock. Joe relaxes and thanks Carmen for the good work. Carmen feels appreciated, compliments Mary for putting in the extra hour of work last night, and reminds her gently of the deadline. Mary, in turn, treats the customer with a cheerful attitude, and he thinks, "What a nice atmosphere this must be to work in."

Giving feedback is needed in the running of any effective organization. When we give feedback with rapport and permission, we not only make the adjustments necessary, we also increase the general feelings of goodwill, morale, and teamwork.

An important key to all workplace relationships is to be able to first keep your own bearings—to live above the line yourself. When we live in a state of mental health, we are able to have cooperation, coordination, and synergy—a recipe for good teamwork.

MEETINGS: GETTING IN THE WAY OF WORK OR HELPING YOU GET YOUR JOB DONE?

Meetings serve several purposes: to communicate new ideas, goals, and information; to inspire and motivate employees; to solve problems; to come to a consensus on policies, projects, and new directions; or to build teamwork on a particular task. A well-run meeting is enjoyable and effective in achieving its purposes, and it leaves people feeling energized, motivated, and positive toward one another. On the other hand, an ineffective meeting is draining, leaves people feeling more distant from each other, and doesn't meet its objectives. What's the difference between an effective and an ineffective meeting?

Many people in organizations have complained to us that one of the worst parts of their job is sitting through the many long and unproductive meetings. The tone of these meetings is usually polite, with nothing getting accomplished, or argumentative, with people leaving angry, distant, and uncooperative. Most unproductive meetings are run in the analytical mode of thinking. When this happens, few people truly listen to one another. Instead, participants are simply waiting for a chance to interrupt or to share their opinion. A sarcastic joke in the corporate world suggests that in meetings such as these, you might as well have only one person show up, because everyone knows ahead of time what will be said anyway!

Keep in mind that in analytical thinking we are operating exclusively out of memory; rarely do new thoughts emerge. Discussions tend to be circular, ego based, and one sided. The result is that there is often a high degree of boredom, distraction, and side talking.

In an effective, inspired meeting, people are operating above the line. The tone is positive, respectful, and open. Everyone is listening more than speaking or waiting to speak. What allows this to happen is that participants are generally in the free-flowing mode of thinking, which facilitates good listening skills and a flow of creative and responsive thinking. It encourages people to see points of agreement and commonality. When participants in a meeting are in the free-flowing mode, their individual opinions, beliefs, and need to prove themselves tend to disappear.

In effectively run meetings, people tend to leapfrog each other's ideas—not in competition, but in a way that improves on each idea, thus moving the discussion toward clarity and unity. Obviously, there will be times you will need the processing mode; you will need to recall relevant information, perform computations, or plan. In general, however, the participants will stay in the creative intelligence mode. Let's take a look at the guidelines for keeping a meeting above the line, in free-flowing thinking:

1. Keep the tone positive, upbeat, and open—flowing. (You may want to appoint a "mood monitor" to let the group know when they are losing the proper tone.)
2. Look for areas of agreement rather than disagreement. Disagreement will happen, but it shouldn't bog down the meeting.

3. Listen in a way that if thoughts do come to mind, you let them go; don't try to hang on to thoughts, or it will stop the listening process.

4. Be curious rather than critical or judgmental about other people's ideas. This will draw them and you deeper into the free-flowing mode.

5. Accept not knowing as a viable option. Recognize when you, or the group as a whole, don't have an answer at the moment, and trust that one will come.

Not everyone works—or even wants to work—in a job where meetings are run above the line. What do you do if you're the only person who understands analytical versus free-flowing thinking? The answer is, even if only one person in a meeting stays in the free-flowing mode, it will have a calming, positive influence on the entire group. If you can listen from the reflective mode while everyone else is bogged down in analytical thinking, you will have a calming effect on the rest of the group. Common denominators will begin to emerge, or you will have insights that can help transcend the differences being presented in the group. One person who maintains perspective and a sense of calm can emerge as a leader or positive influence in the group.

CONSIDER THE POSSIBILITY

The next time you are in a meeting, suggest appointing a "mood monitor." If that isn't appropriate or possible, secretly do it yourself and watch what happens to the productivity of the meeting when the mood drops.

MAKING DECISIONS

How do we make a decision that, over the long run, will prove to be wise? How do we make a decision when there are so many uncertain variables, such as the future marketability of a product? How do we trust a gut feeling about something? Is there any way that we can be assured that we are making the right decision? How do we stay above the line while making decisions?

Certainly having as much information as is possible is a good idea before making any decision. Gathering the facts is important. Unfortunately, all the marketing research, diagnostic information, and input from other significant parties or experts is still not enough, at times, to provide all the information needed to make a sound decision. It's imperative for a decision maker to know how to use both process and free-flowing modes of thinking in order to make the best possible decisions.

The process mode of thinking is sufficient for making a decision where all the variables are known: Do I have enough money left in my budget to send George to get the training he needs? Decisions like these are no-brainers: just feed in the information, and out comes the answer.

When we are faced with a difficult decision, however, we often don't have all the information available, either because it isn't immediately accessible or it doesn't yet exist. For these decisions, we are wise to use our free-flowing mode of thinking. The free-flowing mode is a deep source of intelligence that takes into account all the knowns—and the unknowns—and comes up with a decision that feels right. Some people call this a sense of knowing. Joe's father, who died in 1995, was a very successful entrepreneur. He had a keen ability to study a subject and see the obvious solution to very complex issues. He was often the only person who saw it the way he did, but he was very confident of his decisions. And he was right a vast majority of the time. At his funeral, most of the eulogizers spoke of his decision-making abilities. When people would ask him how he knew what farm to buy or how many trees of a specific variety they should plant this year, he would usually respond with a simple answer such as, "It's just common sense." Common sense was his way of talking about creative intelligence.

Exactly how do we go about using the free-flowing mode for decision making? Three steps are involved in gaining access to the free-flowing mode:

1. *Admit you don't know the answer.* This takes humility and not caring what people will think about your not having an immediate answer on a particular topic. Not knowing is the entry point to the free-flowing mode. Feeling pressure to know kicks your analytical mode into gear and encourages you to get caught up in your thinking.

2. *Feed any known variables and any questions that occur to you to the back burner.* For example, suppose you are trying to decide which candidate would be the best person to hire for a key position in your organization. To use your back burner, ask yourself questions like, "What kind of person do we need for this job? What qualities are most important for this position? How will this person do under pressure?"

You will certainly do a responsible search for the right candidate, interviewing each of them—probably several times—and performing extensive background checks and references. Once you have all of the information, however, rather than churning the facts over and over in your head, you simply put it on the back burner of your mind and forget about it. Each time the issue comes back into your mind, gently put it back on the back burner again, until you have a strong sense of knowing. Knowing is a level of certainty that won't come from analysis; it's a feeling that can come only from the free-flowing mode. You can even tell your back burner your time deadline. Your back burner will take that variable into consideration as well.

3. *Remember that your ability to use the back burner is directly related to how much faith you have in the free-flowing mode.* Using your back burner effectively is about letting go and is directly related to living above the line.

Let's illustrate this process with an example. John is the manager of a division for an engineering company and needs to hire a new project manager for the biggest growth area for the company. After six months of interviews, reference checks, and meetings with his staff, there is conflict among the staff members about who is the best candidate. John must make the ultimate decision. He has a weekend planned to go fishing, and he decides he will reflect on the decision while he's away from the office.

John understands that reflecting means not churning about the decision but rather letting it come in and out of his mind while he is in a relaxed mode of thinking. As he gets deeper into his free-flowing mode, as he becomes more relaxed, he realizes his decision; he arrives at a strong sense of knowing about it. He feels confident in presenting his decision to his team when he returns. Decisions need not be the product of sleepless nights but of a calm, clear certainty.

DEALING WITH DEADLINES

We have waited until the last section of the book to write about deadlines. Maybe we are procrastinating about deadlines like so many in the workplace! It is not uncommon for the number one cause of stress in the workplace to be deadlines. Why are deadlines so difficult to deal with? Why do we seem to wait till the last possible moment to sit down and write that report or turn in that memo? In this section we will look at two kinds of deadlines—externally imposed and internally imposed. We will look at procrastination and how to prevent it. We will learn how to stay out of process mode and in free-flowing mode when it comes to deadlines.

People complain about two kinds of deadlines—those that are internally imposed and those that are externally imposed. To some people the one is more difficult to deal with, to some the other. As we discussed in an earlier chapter, the experience of pressure—and stress—is all a result of unhealthy thinking. It's how we think about deadlines that determines if they are a challenge, a pain, or terrifying.

Joe recently interviewed several employees who work in an accounting division of a large company. He asked each of them how stressful deadlines were to them and how the division dealt with them. Each person responded quite differently, according to their level of understanding. Those below the line saw deadlines as very stressful and took them very personally—as though supervisors were being inconsiderate. Those living above the line saw that there were certain very predictable times of the year when more demands were made on them and they needed to work more hours, but they didn't see those times as stressful, just more demanding. Perception equals experience.

Life is always happening only one moment at a time. However, as most of us have experienced, we can be thinking about a million things at the same time. When we do this, we lose concentration, get easily distracted, and fail to complete tasks. This is the nature of procrastination—doing one thing and thinking about another.

The cure for procrastination and for dealing with the pressure of deadlines is to operate, as much as possible, in the free-flowing mode. When we are in the free-flowing mode and have a lot to do in a short amount of time, we shift into a different gear and become extremely focused, efficient, and creative at our work. Some people call this being "in the zone." When we are in the zone, we can do enormous amounts of work in a short time, yet with a higher level of quality than normal.

SUMMARY

In this chapter we have focused on the world of work—how to work smarter. We began by defining working smarter as working in a way that is in the moment, wiser, and less frenetic. We looked at how to be more efficient, balanced, and creative. We described how levels of understanding translate into the world of work and organizations. The lower the level of understanding, the more difficult and stressful all the operations of work become—time management, relationships, decision making, meetings, and deadlines. As the understanding of employees moves above the line, we saw how work becomes more productive, fun, and creative with less energy—true success. We discussed applying what we have learned in this book to time management, relationships, moods, giving feedback, running meetings effectively, decision making, and dealing with deadlines. We hope this will help you to work smarter and enjoy your life more in the process.

CHAPTER 8

Enjoying Life

Not long ago Richard was jogging by a tennis court where two men were finishing up a game. One said to the other, "I'm giving up this game; I'm just not getting any better." The other replied, "But I thought you loved the game of tennis." The first responded, "I do, but so what? Loving the game isn't getting me anywhere." Sadly, this is the attitude of many people who might otherwise love their leisure activities. If something isn't leading them somewhere (wherever that might be), then it must not be worth doing.

One of the most stressful times for many people is when they are on vacation or at leisure. As a culture we have far more free or leisure time than at any time in the world's civilization. Yet what we have done is to take our centuries-old work ethic and transfer it our leisure time. It's common to see people tossing their golf clubs, tennis rackets, or fishing poles in disgust because their performance isn't meeting their hopes or expectations. It's also common for people to choose a leisure activity based as much on their ability to improve as on how much they really enjoy the activity.

A personal story demonstrates the stress we can create for ourselves even on vacation. Richard just returned from an out-of-state trip with some very close friends. These particular friends tend to try to cram as much as possible into their vacation time. Each family has two children, and by the time they returned home all four kids (as well as Richard and his wife) were exhausted. Their two friends had scheduled virtually every moment of every day—one activity after another, after another. They went from historic buildings to museums to train rides through the countryside to swimming pools to restaurants to more tourist locations and back to the hotel. Then, when everyone finally had a moment to relax, these friends were immediately on the phone or looking through magazines planning the next thing and the next and the next. It seemed that they were always asking, "What do you want to do next?" But when Richard answered by saying, "Nothing," or "We'd rather just hang out," they appeared disappointed, as if everyone wasn't getting the most out of their time together—as if doing things were the important thing. The more activities the better.

What makes this overactive scheduling so stressful is not only the amount of activity involved, it's also the tendency that comes with busyness to be focused not on the moment at hand but on the moments yet to be—what we're going to be doing next, and later, and tomorrow. When your mind is operating in this future-oriented manner, the amount of satisfaction you can receive from any single experience is severely limited. Your ability to feel satisfied with your experiences is directly tied to how present you are able to be.

Remember, thoughts are feelings. Therefore, if you are having frenetic, busy thinking, you will be having frenetic, agitated feelings.

This was obviously the case for the people on Richard's vacation. Everyone's mind was so preoccupied with what was coming next that no one felt nourished by the experiences taking place in the present. Looking back, Richard remembers many conversations that were filled up with comments like, "Tomorrow is going to be fun," and "Where do you want to have dessert?"

Please don't misinterpret our message. There's nothing inherently wrong with planning or speculating about the future—it's often important, useful, or interesting. The problem arises when your present moments are filled up with futuristic thinking or with thinking that is removed from this moment. The further your attention is from this moment, the more stress you will feel and the less pleasure you will experience.

SATISFACTION

There is a direct correlation between the degree to which you are in the present moment and the number of experiences you need to feel satisfied. The less present you are, the more activities you will need to feel a sense of satisfaction. This means that if you are oriented to the present moment, you'll need very few activities to make you feel as though you are getting enough from life and from your experiences. Each experience will tend to be rich and fulfilling. For instance, you won't need to travel the world or go to Disneyland to feel as though your experiences are meeting your needs. Instead, you'll feel satisfied taking a peaceful walk in the woods close to home. Your present-moment orientation will allow you to fill your spirit with the beauty around you, to notice the sights, sounds, and smells of your surroundings. You may still decide to travel the world and do varied and exciting things, but you won't feel ripped off or disappointed if you can't.

On the other end the scale, if you are not oriented to the present moment—if your thinking usually focuses on past or future experiences—you'll rarely feel filled up by any single experience. You'll constantly need more and more experiences to feel satisfied. Walking in the park will never be enough; you'll have to be scheduling a skiing trip while you're walking or thinking about something else that would make life more enjoyable than it is right now. Your lack of orientation to the present moment will prevent you from taking in the pleasant sights, sounds, and feelings of your experience. Your mind will be somewhere other than in this moment.

The point here is not to say that fewer activities are better or that the goal is to eliminate excitement from your life. Rather, it's to point out that the reason most of us feel compelled to fill each moment with varied and continued activities is because we aren't satisfied with what we are experiencing. If you were satisfied, why would you bother rushing around, searching for what would be even better? The root reason we aren't satisfied is because our attention is rarely in the moment. Instead of living at the speed of life, we move too quickly. Consequently, we miss what we already have—right in front of us—and look for something else. It's almost as though we'd rather be anywhere other than where we are.

TAKING YOUR LIFE WITH YOU

Richard remembers the first time that he and his wife took a few days away from their kids, just for themselves. They had dreamed of this special time for more than a year. They planned their getaway to a romantic, peaceful town on the northern California coast.

While they were driving away from home, and for the entire first day, they talked about—you guessed it—their kids! Neither one of them was in touch with the present moment; the first day happened without any awareness or thought recognition. The entire reason for the two of them to be going away together was to get away from the kids, to be alone. But there they were, away from the kids, in one of the most beautiful spots on earth, and all they were doing was spending time with the kids in their minds and in their conversations. They wondered about how the kids were doing and whether or not they were having fun. They talked about family time, family vacations that were over, fond memories of when the kids were little, and everything else you can possibly imagine—all about the kids.

About the middle of the second day, Richard's wife, Kris, said in a startled voice, "Do you realize that we have been away for more than twenty-four hours, and all we have done is take our life with us? We've talked about nothing other than the kids." Both Kris and Richard were shocked at what they had been doing, and after laughing at themselves for a while, they both committed themselves to trying to stay more in the moments they were having—in the present. The rest of their trip was far more interesting and intimate now that they were focused on each other and on their time together.

SATISFACTION IN THE PRESENT MOMENT

The most important moment of your life is this one—right now! Truly it's the only moment that you have. All other moments are either over and are now just a memory, or they are yet to be—a mere speculative thought about some future moment.

Being in the moment and feeling inspired by what you are experiencing are linked in an important way. When you are fully present in the moment—when you are deeply immersed in what you are doing—you will feel filled up and inspired by each experience. It will take relatively few experiences to make you feel as though life itself is rich and fulfilling. Each new experience will fill you with wonder and delight; each one will be special.

However, the opposite is also true. When your mind is not in the moment—when it's scattered or focused on what's next or when you're comparing your present experience to other experiences you have had—you have removed the very thing that makes enjoyment possible. Your attention is the mechanism leading to the feeling of satisfaction. It is only when your mind is engaged in the moment that you will feel that what you are experiencing is enough.

To return, for a moment, to our story about Richard's vacation with his friends, you can easily see that people were not feeling satisfied. Whatever they were doing clearly wasn't good enough; they had to be doing something else, something better, something more interesting—more, more, more. But clearly the cause of everyone's dissatisfaction couldn't have been the activities themselves; many people dream of doing the supposedly fun things they were doing on that trip.

The problem was that Richard and his friends weren't in the present moment, fully enjoying their vacation. If they had been, they would have been comfortable slowing down and having fewer experiences yet getting more out of each one. The mistake everyone made was continuing to look outside of themselves for the great experience that was going to fill them up, rather than recognizing that their experiences were each potentially nourishing and fulfilling in and of themselves. Their lack of present-moment orientation kept them from the enjoyment they were seeking.

RED FLAGS

There are four red flags, or cues, to alert you when your mind has drifted away from the present moment during leisure time. They are:

1. *You feel bored—as if something else would be much more interesting.* Boredom is a clear indicator that your mind has drifted away from this moment to what would be better or more interesting. Or to what was better or more interesting. When your mind is focused on what would be better, it makes what you are actually experiencing seem dull. I was recently at a beautiful reservoir eating my lunch, when I overheard two men complaining about being bored. They were discussing how much more fun it would be if they could only be back in Hawaii, apparently where they had just been on vacation. Think about what they were doing to themselves. Here they were sitting together, two friends under a beautiful oak tree on a gorgeous, warm, sunny day, with ducks and other birds swimming right in front of them. And they were bored stiff, longing to be somewhere else!

Their minds were on Hawaii, an experience that was over and done with.

2. *You get overly absorbed in planning future moments.* If you notice yourself spending your leisure time planning your next leisure time, beware! It suggests that you're in your head, removed from the moment, instead of operating in the free-flowing mode. Remember, it's almost impossible to relax and enjoy yourself in the present moment if the bulk of your attention is on the question "What's next?" When this happens, gently bring your attention back to the here and now.

3. *You're unusually tired, even though you thought you were relaxing.* Part of the reason for enjoying leisure time is to rejuvenate your body and spirit. If you're on vacation or out enjoying the weekend and you're feeling really tired, it may suggest that you are moving too fast or doing too many things. It might be time to slow down and relax. Remember Richard's vacation, where he and his family returned far more tired than when they had left! Sometimes, however, if you have been speeded up—living at too quick a pace—and you slow down to the speed of life, you will initially feel tired, even exhausted. In these instances, you may need to catch up on your sleep until you feel rested and rejuvenated.

4. *You're frustrated, even though you're (supposedly) out enjoying yourself.* When you're mad at yourself because your tennis game isn't as good as you would like it to be, or when you're otherwise frustrated during leisure time, it's a good indication that your mind is busy comparing how you are playing today with how you played last week or how you think you should be playing. This can be called "the comparison trap." Your mind isn't in the moment, enjoying the game; it's out of the moment comparing itself to another, completely

different experience. As you remember that each experience is unique unto itself and you bring your full attention to the experience you are actually having, your frustration will diminish and your enjoyment will increase.

THE MECHANICS OF ENJOYMENT

Let's take a look at a few common activities that almost everyone enjoys and see what they have in common:

- Making love
- Reading a thoughtful letter
- Rock climbing, river rafting, or engaging in some other exhilarating activity
- Watching a moving film or reading a exciting or emotional book

On the surface, the above activities are very different. There appears to be no similarity between making love and reading a good book. But at a different level, the two can be very similar. And once you take note of the similarity, you can begin to have more appreciation for—and get more pure enjoyment out of—virtually any activity, leisure or otherwise.

When you are making love, your mind is rarely somewhere else. Instead, you are extremely present, fully engaged in what you are doing. Losing yourself in a heartfelt letter or movie often creates the same experience. The more absorbed within the pages you are, the more intense is the experience of your book. You may have had the experience of not hearing someone who was trying to get your attention while you were reading. You were so engrossed in the words on the page that you blocked out many of the sights and sounds that might normally distract you. During these moments of full concentration, it's almost as if your book is the entire world—it's all that matters. When people speak of escaping into a book, they are referring to being totally absorbed in the story. Yet the same attention can be devoted to the moments of your life. Being in the reflective mode is all that is required to be totally absorbed in the story of your life.

Can you imagine what would happen if, in the middle of making love, you said to your partner, "Honey, do you remember where I put my briefcase?" You (and your partner) would lose most, if not all, of your enjoyment and connection. The distraction would take you away (in your mind) from where you were and what you were doing. The same would be true while reading a heartfelt letter from someone you love. What would happen if, instead of concentrating on what you were reading, you stopped every two seconds to think about someone you were angry at? Very simply, you'd ruin your present-moment experience. You would be distracted.

You can probably guess that if an experience itself, like the heartfelt letter, were the actual cause of your satisfaction, then your scattered attention would have no impact on you. You'd receive the same joy whether you were focused or distracted, whether you were present or absent. But we know this isn't the case. We've found that it's our concentration— our ability to stay in the moment, focused on what we are doing—that allows us to enjoy the positive feelings of our experiences. The more present we are, the more positive our feelings, the more joy and satisfaction we will experience and receive.

EXHILARATING EXPERIENCES

A good friend of Richard's is an excellent rock climber. He once took Richard on a beautiful and challenging climb in the Yosemite Valley. It was one of the most exhilarating experiences of Richard's life. Despite assurances that he would be safe, Richard was petrified as he looked down the sheer cliff that they were trying to climb. Richard vividly remembers his intense concentration, how each step and each rock seemed to come alive. To this day, he's not quite sure how he made it safely to the top, but somehow it happened.

After the climb, Richard asked his friend why he loved climbing so much. The answer, which was offered with enthusiastic conviction, has always stuck with him: "I climb because when I'm climbing it's almost impossible *not* to be present. I must be right where I am and nowhere else. This brings me great joy and allows me to bring this type of attention to some of the rest of my life." The friend's answer makes a great deal of sense. During the climb, Richard's attention was not on his work, his children or family, what he was going to have for dinner, or any worries or concerns. Instead, his full attention was on just the step he was working on, and nothing else.

Richard has told this story to clients, several of whom have said, "I see what you're saying, but that kind of focus would be easy when your life is on the line. What about more ordinary activities?"

It's been our experience and the experience of many that we have worked with that we can learn how to be every bit as oriented to the present moment in our more ordinary leisure activities as we can be when we're climbing a mountain, sailing a boat, skiing down a mountain, or riding a wave. Ultimately, what brings joy to any experience isn't the experience itself but the quality of thinking that we bring to it.

What some of these extraordinary activities do is *force* us to be oriented to the present moment in our thinking. When you climb a mountain, you really can't afford to be thinking about your son's poor grades in school. When you're taking a walk, however, you can get away with thinking about three or four things at once without jeopardizing your life. But what you do jeopardize is the quality of your experience. The next time you're taking a walk, jogging, or drawing a picture, see if you can notice how often your mind drifts to other things. As you let go of unnecessary thinking, you'll discover a wealth of joy in the simplest of moments.

LEARNING FROM CHILDREN

One day, as Richard was taking one of his daughters to the beach, he had some minor tire trouble, so he stopped at the service station to have it repaired. While Richard and his daughter waited, they walked across the street to play at the park. Within a few minutes Richard began to get impatient. He looked at his watch. His mind was on his plan—the beach. He began urging his daughter to come back with him to the car so that they could drive to the beach and "have some fun." Richard started saying things like, "Come on, sweetie. Think about how much fun we're going to have." At the time, her response surprised him, but in retrospect, it made a great deal of sense. She said, in no uncertain terms, "I don't want to go. I want to stay here." Her obvious feeling was: Why in the world should I get back in a hot car and drive for two hours (each way) so that I can have fun, when I'm already here in a beautiful shady park, having a blast with my dad and other kids? This is not to say that it's never appropriate or important to stick to your original plan if it's something you truly want to experience—or if you feel it's important for your child to experience. But think about it for a minute. A two-year-old girl is smiling in a sandy park, playing and laughing with other children, completely absorbed and joyful in what she is already doing. She's making sand castles, pouring water, and climbing on play structures. How could anything possibly be more fun than that? Her dad, however, can't stop thinking about his plan to go to the beach! Rather than sharing in his daughter's incredible and visible joy, he's focused on something that is going to be even better.

Generally speaking, children are masters of living in the present, but it's easy to squelch this tendency. Innocently, without even knowing it, we teach them that "someday life will be better" or "right now isn't good enough"—the message Richard's daughter was getting from him.

Being able to immerse yourself in the here and now is magical. As you do, a renewed sense of gratitude and awe begins to resurface in your life. We've already seen that present-moment living is an antidote to worry, concern, frustration, and regret. What we see through examples such as these is that present-moment living is also the key to enjoying and appreciating the leisure part of your life.

A QUIET MIND

If you want to experience more joy, it's important to quiet your mind so that you can stay focused in the moment. You probably already know what a busy mind feels like: over-whelmed, heavy, and concerned. A busy mind has no room for creativity and fresh thought. It's too busy and hurried, evaluating everyone's performance, especially its own. It tends to go over the same set of facts and problems over and over until it reaches some sort of decision, which is often similar to a decision it made before. It then rushes on to the next set of facts and does the very same thing. A person with an overly busy mind is incapable of enjoying life, even leisure time, because a busy mind cannot stay in the moment; it is usually wondering how it is doing, or it's on to the next thing.

BOREDOM

One of the major reasons we resist slowing down to the speed of life is that we are frightened of becoming bored. We feel that if we keep moving quickly, doing a lot of things, boredom will never become a problem. Understanding the actual causes of boredom can help you feel comfortable in slowing down your life, and it can help you increase the joy you experience in your leisure time.

Boredom is one of the trickiest areas of modern life to deal with because it appears to be something that it is not. Boredom has nothing to do with not having enough to do and everything to do with having an overactive, busy mind.

Think back to the last time you sat in front of a beautiful roaring fire with someone you love. You may have sat for hours, contented, absorbed in each special moment. Clearly, you were not doing much, your mind was clear and free, you were in a healthy thought process—you were anything but bored. The truth is, whenever you are in this free-flowing mode, oriented to the present moment, you feel satisfied; life is just right. A key to enjoying and appreciating all of your leisure time is not to spend more time in front of fires, but to learn to gain access to this healthy thought process.

Now think back to the last time you were stuck in traffic. You may have been caught for only a few minutes, yet you were probably bored stiff, right? Far more was going on around you than was going on in front of the fireplace, yet boredom set in, in a matter of minutes.

Why? Because as you sit in traffic your mind begins to rush around to all the places you'd rather be and all the things you'd rather be doing. Rather than sitting quietly and experiencing the moment (as you would do in your free-flowing or creative mode), your analytical mind plunges toward the future: "How am I going to get out of this?" Or it shoots backward to the past: "How did I get myself into this?" You allow your mind to speed up and fill up to the point of an unhealthy thought process. The busier your mind gets, the further you move away from the present moment and the less satisfaction you feel.

In front of the fireplace, your mind was relatively free from distraction. Your thoughts were flowing, and your mind was clear. Because there wasn't an overabundance of thought in your head, you were able to enjoy something as simple as a roaring fire. You had slowed down to the speed of life. As your head fills up with excess thoughts, however, your ability to enjoy the moment is removed. This dynamic will happen wherever you are. As your mind fills with concerns and worries, moving further away from the present moment, you become less able to enjoy yourself and your children, even on vacation. You can be in the most beautiful place on earth, doing wonderful things, but if your mind is overactive, you won't be able to see the beauty around you. You'll be too busy evaluating what you are seeing, or you will be thinking about something else.

The next time you feel bored, notice the quantity of thought or level of mental activity in your head. The more overactive your mind is, the less able you will be to enjoy your life. When you see or feel the signs of a busy mind (boredom setting in), keep in mind what is really causing the boredom—a busy mind, not lack of activity.

Consider what would happen to your positive experience of sitting in front of the fire if your mind started worrying about something. Within a matter of seconds, you would be wishing you were somewhere else, doing something different. Satisfaction would disappear. Your mind would be so busy— you would feel you needed things to do—that you would think that taking action would bring you greater satisfaction. Once you began doing something else, though, your mind would start the process all over again. A never-ending cycle of dissatisfaction begins when your mind keeps telling you something else will bring you joy.

The solution to boredom is to stay more in the present moment. When your mind is immersed in the present moment, not overly busy, boredom doesn't exist! You could be busy as a bee or just hanging out doing nothing. The activity itself isn't relevant; in fact, it makes no difference at all.

LEARNING TO RELAX

People who enjoy their leisure time and who have learned to relax experience moments when nothing is on their minds.

They welcome these moments, because such moments open the door for inspiration. Happy, relaxed people use these quiet moments to gain access to wisdom and creativity—as a vehicle to tell them what to do next. People who have learned to slow down to the speed of life know intuitively that creativity is a process that bubbles up inside them automatically when their mind is clear and quiet. They know they don't have to figure out what to do next; something will just occur to them. Those moments when your mind is free of distraction are the very moments when you have the greatest potential for creativity.

If you frequently experience boredom, you might think that a quiet mind is boring. The very thought of having nothing to do may cause panic, leading you to quickly create something to replace the quiet. Consequently, your mind is almost never quiet; almost anything is better than doing nothing. Your unconscious goal may be to fill every moment of your life with some kind of activity. How many of us can sit, even for two minutes, without doing something?

Occasionally, when people hear us advocating having "nothing on your mind," fear sets in that they will stop being productive. You can rest assured that if you learn to relax, if you can accept the value of having nothing on your mind, you will be plenty productive, probably even more so.

The willingness to have a clear or empty mind ensures that you will never again experience boredom. When you learn to welcome those infrequent moments when nothing much is on your mind, you will increase the awe and wonder in your life; the smallest things will bring you joy. You will begin to see aspects of life that were previously invisible, because your mind will no longer be filled up with the old, and it will be receptive to newness.

GRAZING

A helpful analogy for trying to understand the essence of a quiet mind is to think of horses grazing in a field. Horses wander around looking for food. They don't focus on any one area for very long; they drift from place to place.

So too with a quiet mind. It doesn't focus on any one thought—or series of thoughts—for too long. Thoughts come, then flow out. Not much attention is given to any single thought. All thoughts are treated equally. A quiet mind is a mind at rest, like an animal grazing in a field.

In these quiet moments, you will be pleasantly surprised with frequent inspirations and insights that will delight you—thoughts like "That's what I need to do" or "That's so obvious." You will find new solutions to important questions that you may have been struggling with. Life will seem easier, more manageable. Your relaxation time will actually become relaxing!

RUNNING IN NEUTRAL

One major purpose of leisure time is to allow the mind to relax. Just as the body needs sleep, so too does the mind. It needs time to be empty, not in active use. It needs time in the free-flowing mode, slowed down to the speed of life.

If you think of the gears of a car, neutral is the gear of rest. In neutral, the car can still be on, but it's not being actively used. It's ready to go, if needed, on a moment's notice, but in the meantime it's in a state of rest.

You can think of a calm, relaxed mind in a similar light. When the mind is at rest, it is not in active gear. A mind in neutral is still operating, taking in information, computing on its back burner, but in a relaxed, passive mode. Instead of focusing or analyzing, it allows thoughts to enter and leave. They come in, and they go out. Like meditative states, neutral is a state of rest, but unlike meditation, neutral can be called upon anytime, anyplace, with your eyes open, fully alert.

While neutral is a state of mind that can be used to relax and rejuvenate at practically any time, leisure time is an ideal place to experiment. If you spend more time in neutral, you'll quickly discover that you are much easier to satisfy. Ordinary, everyday things will seem somehow extraordinary.

Richard remembers when he was first introduced to the concept of neutral. He was studying with a teacher, Dr. George Pransky, in La Conner, Washington. At the time, his mind was in a constantly busy state. He was used to filling up each moment with lots of activity. The problem was, there's not much to do in La Conner, in the normal sense of things to do. There is no theater, no nightlife to speak of, little excitement. Richard asked Dr. Pransky, "What's there to do around here at night?" The teacher's answer has always stuck with him. After introducing Richard to the concept of neutral, he said to him, "I'd really like it if, for just one night, you would simply do nothing, allow yourself to be bored. Don't drive to Seattle, don't talk on the phone, and don't go find a theater or even watch TV." Richard thought he was kidding! Why in the world would anyone intentionally become bored?

Because he was in La Conner to learn from this man, however, Richard took his advice to heart and did his best to comply. And to his absolute amazement, it was one of the most beautiful evenings of his entire life! As soon as he allowed

himself to be bored—as soon as he stopped being so frightened of boredom and stopped fighting it—his mind cleared
and he was anything but bored. He remembers becoming
more observant of pure, natural beauty than he had ever been
in his life. He was drawn to take a quiet walk, all by himself,
something he had rarely done before. He remembers bending
down to look at insects that he had never before noticed. He
was also in awe of the tulips that he was seeing. Prior to this
introduction to the value of a mind in neutral, he hadn't even
noticed that there were flowers in La Conner! Richard's mind
was so busy thinking about other things, so out of touch with
the present moment, that he had completely failed to see the
beauty right in front of his eyes.

BRINGING LEISURE TO THE REST OF YOUR LIFE

We hope that after reading this chapter you will be able to
bring more joy and relaxation to the leisure part of your life.
By slowing down to the speed of life, you will become more
oriented to the present moment in your leisure time, more
focused, and, where wanted or needed, more proficient. Less
leisure time will be required to bring forth full and complete
relaxation, and you will be much more easily satisfied by the
leisure that your time and other circumstances allow.

A final thought to consider: As you learn to quiet your
mind and become more oriented to the present moment during your leisure activities, you will begin to bring the feeling
of leisure into the rest of your life. Rather than dichotomizing
your life into work versus leisure, you'll begin to bring them
closer together. You'll find that a little bit of leisure does, in
fact, go a long way. You'll being to take the same focused,

calm, and relaxed mind-set that you are using in your leisure life and apply it to other parts of your life as well. Hopefully, you'll discover what the two of us have discovered: It's not what you're doing that brings you joy as much as it is a relaxed mind-set. When your mind is calm, your entire life will seem calmer.

RESOURCES

To receive a catalog listing additional information on Psychology of Mind, including other books and tapes, call 541–383–9362 or write to Psychology of Mind Resource Center, 2436 N.W. Torsway, Bend, OR 97701.

Website: www.psychologyofmind.com

For training and seminars, call the POM Foundation at 1–800–781–2066, or write to them at 1111 Third Avenue West, Suite 350, Bradenton, FL 34240.